Understanding the Faith

& the Challenges of Today

Michael A. Garcia

authorHOUSE®

AuthorHouse™
1663 Liberty Drive
Bloomington, IN 47403
www.authorhouse.com
Phone: 1 (800) 839-8640

Nihil Obstat:
Msgr. Chanel Jeanty

Imprimatur:
+Thomas Wenski, Archbishop of Miami
1 December 2015

Book Cover Design by: William Garcia

Published by AuthorHouse 04/21/2017

ISBN: 978-1-5246-8615-4 (sc)
ISBN: 978-1-5246-8613-0 (hc)
ISBN: 978-1-5246-8614-7 (e)

Library of Congress Control Number: 2017905197

Print information available on the last page.

Any people depicted in stock imagery provided by Thinkstock are models,
and such images are being used for illustrative purposes only.
Certain stock imagery © Thinkstock.

This book is printed on acid-free paper.

For the men and women who have dedicated their lives to seminary formation, and for my family.

Contents

Part I
The Historical Narrative

Part II
The Christian of Today

Part I

The Historical Narrative

The Fall

Introduction

"Why study the faith?" A fair question, indeed. To study the Catholic faith is to study who we are, where we come from, and what our purpose in life is. These questions are intricately embedded in what we believe. The object of this book is to have a better understanding of who we are and what role we play in this drama we now call "Salvation History." In order to do this we must start at the very beginning. In order to know where we are going we must first look at where we came from. This includes looking at a brief history of the people of Israel up to the point of the Christ Event. From there, we will take a look at the life, teachings and sacraments of Christ. Finally, we will explore what it means to live a life *in* Christ. "Why must we live the Christian life?" you might ask. The answer: because to be fully human *is* to live a life in Christ. Anything else would be inauthentic to who we are. The more we deviate from the teachings of Christ, the less human and less authentic we become. The goal is to show that we are part of something bigger than ourselves, something that requires full and active participation, something that leads to ultimate happiness and freedom. We dare not strive for anything less!

Every story has a starting point. As J. R. R. Tolkien once wrote: "There cannot be any 'story' without a fall – all stories are ultimately about the fall."[1] Ours is not so different. We too begin with a fall. Ours begins in the very first book of the Bible known as *Genesis*, which literally means the beginning, and indeed, it is the starting point of the history we call "human drama." What is the Bible? The Bible, simply put, is a collection of divinely inspired books. In fact, the word "Bible" comes from the Greek, *Ta Biblia*, which literally means "the books." The first part of the Bible is called the Old Testament, which is comprised of 46 books. These books are divided into three parts: the Law, the Prophets, and the Sacred Writings. The Law, or the *Torah*, is also known as the Pentateuch in the Latin Church (The Roman Catholic Church). These are the first five books of the Old Testament. It begins with Genesis and ends with Deuteronomy. It is here, in Genesis, where we will take a look at our own fall and the subsequent effects thereof.

Before we enter into the meat of Sacred Scripture it is notable to first discuss the importance of storytelling as a way of conveying truth. Sometimes storytelling is the best way of conveying truth. J.R.R. Tolkien, creator of *The Lord of the Rings*, once wrote: "After all, I believe that legends and myths are largely made of 'truth', and indeed present aspects of it that can only be received in this mode; and long ago certain truths and modes of this kind were discovered and must always reappear."[2] When we were children our parents used to tell us stories to teach us lessons. Many times we were not aware that a lesson was being taught, but somehow, we were able to learn an important truth subconsciously, that is, without being consciously aware of it. Take for example the story of *Snow White*. The lesson or truth of this fairytale was to make known the evils of vanity (the wicked stepmother). Or take for example the story of *Hansel and Gretel*. The story was meant to keep children from falling into gluttony. If you remember the story, Hansel and Gretel were drawn to the wicked witch's cottage because it was made of candy. As it turned out, the witch used the alluring house as a ploy to capture and eat them. Yet, the main purpose of these stories were not so much to question, "did this really happen?" but more importantly, "what was the truth or lesson that I, the reader, was able to learn?"

We must take the same approach when reading Sacred Scripture, especially the first five books of the Old Testament. Like I alluded to before, I am not questioning whether these things actually happened, i.e. historical facts. I am more importantly exploring the truths they convey. As we dive into scripture we will also explore the context (historical & cultural setting) in which they were written and to whom they were written for so we could grasp a more complete understanding of the text.

So, let us start from the beginning. In the beginning God, who is all loving and all knowing, created the heavens and the earth, everything visible and invisible. Surrounding God are a group of spiritual beings known as "angels" or "messengers." This assembly of angelic beings serves God as his delegates and they make up the heavenly court. Unlike God, however, they do not have the power to create things. This is why only God may hold the title of "Creator." Yet, there were some among them who were envious of God's powers. In the history of sin, one sin stands above all others, one sin that would repeatedly change the course of history: pride. One angel, in particular, would fall victim to this sin. This angel sought to deceive others into believing he was the true bearer of light and not God. He boasted, "I will ascend to heaven; above the stars of God I will set my throne on high; I will sit on the mount of assembly in the far north; I will ascend above the heights of the clouds, I will make myself like the Most High" (Is 14:13, NAB). For his insubordination, this angel and his followers were cast out from heaven and into the darkness. These fallen angels, or *demons* as we now call them, will forever be tormented by the mere knowledge that although they sought eternal separation from God, they will never escape the fact that without God they can have no being. For you see, in his benevolence, God made angels, as well as humanity, with free will. He gave us free will so we could freely choose to follow what is good. Sometimes, however, because of our own selfishness, we choose the path not intended by God, but rather the deceivingly more attractive path that leads to destruction and doom.

We thus arrive at *our* story, the story of human drama. God decides to create the physical world, and with it, something so wonderful and so valuable that he even decides to make it in his own image: he creates man, and because "it is not good for man to be alone (Gn 2:18)" he created woman to accompany him. So then, we might ask ourselves, "Why did God create us?" The answer is quite simple: because he loves us. It was because of love and through love that we were created in his image. Therefore, our purpose as human beings is to freely return that love to God. That is why God gave us free will.

As human beings, however, our knowledge is limited. We do not have the capacity to know things as the angels do since they are not confined to the properties of space and time like we are. We are corporeal beings, that is, beings with flesh and blood. We come to know things through the senses and through our rationale (reason), which allows us to recognize such things as goodness, beauty and truth. We therefore are in a pilgrimage of constant discovery. Throughout our lives we use our will and reason with the virtue of faith to navigate through the created things of this world in order to grow in knowledge of God who created them. Therefore, these created things when used appropriately are signs that point us to God himself. Take for example a beautiful landscape or a favorite dish we like to eat. These things please the senses and give us pleasure because in their finite existence they contain goodness, beauty and truth that come from their infinite source, the Creator. Take also the human body. The human body in itself is beautiful, good, and true. The temptation, however, is to hold these created things above the One who created them. In our search for God, we can easily be led astray by turning these things into idols and valuing them above their Creator. We may even make the mistake, as the demons did, of thinking that we can even know more than God.

This brings us to "The Fall," or as some call it, "the sin of origin." As some of you may know, Adam, the first man, and Eve, the first woman, were both tempted by the serpent to eat from the tree of the knowledge between good and evil. God had commanded them to eat anything from the Garden of Eden except from that one specific tree. The temptation here was not of a bodily appetite, but of a different, yet familiar, appetite: the appetite to be like God, the very same that caused the downfall of the demons. This story is trying to convey a truth. Lets take a deeper look at what really happened, for this is not just a story of disobedience, but rather, the greatest tragedy in human history, a tragedy that would only be redeemed by the single greatest act of love the world has ever known. We'll get to that later. Before The Fall, before sin that is, humanity was in perfect union with their Creator. The Garden of Eden was not simply a garden, but a paradise (i.e. an extreme intimacy with God). Keep in mind, that although earthly pleasures may bring us much delight, they only do so because they come from God. Imagine *living* in the presence of that source! Genesis even goes as far as to describe God walking among them in the garden (c.f. Gn 3:8). The Israelites had such an intimate understanding of God that they used to believe that the reason human beings could live was because they literally breathed in God's spirit. The cost of gaining this knowledge of good and evil was unfortunately this intimate union. "How?" you might ask. The answer lies in the nature of the temptation. The serpent said: "You will not die. For God knows when you eat of it, your eyes will be opened, and you will be like God, knowing good and evil" (Gn 3:5). The temptation, my friends, is to abandon our trust in God in pursuit of acquiring (or better yet, stealing) divine knowledge in order to make *ourselves* gods, to deceive ourselves into believing we know more than God, and thus also come to the belief that we no longer need Him. This temptation still occurs today. The continuous removal of God from today's society is a testament to that.

Upon eating the fruit from the tree, Adam and Eve's eyes were opened and they realized they were naked. What does this mean? Did they not know they were naked before? The story is once again trying to convey a deeper truth. Their eyes were opened: they now know what evil is; their innocence was lost. Evil, according to St. Augustine, is nothing more than the absence of the good. Because of their actions, Adam and Eve strayed away from the goodness of God in pursuit of their own agenda. When we step away from what is good we naturally arrive at what is not good, i.e. evil. Hence, for the first time, humanity became aware, gained knowledge that is, of what is evil. The serpent, therefore, did not lie to Adam and Eve. He did promise that in turning away from God's command they would acquire this "knowledge" of evil.

They knew that they were naked: They became exposed. With their newfound knowledge they were able to see the world, and each other, without the inherent goodness contained therein. Because of the nature of who they are (corporeal beings), sin was able to evolve,

7

or rather, expand into every aspect of their livelihood. Hence, we have the introduction of greed, envy, vanity, lust and every other evil that occurs in our world today. Because they sought separation from God, Adam and Eve lost paradise. How can God allow this to happen? Ironically, he allowed it to happen because he loves us. In his love, God gave humanity free will so that humanity can love Him back freely. God knew that by granting humanity free will he was taking the risk of being rejected. One could only imagine the disappointment God felt (and continues to feel) when his own children no longer desire Him.

The Covenants

A rift occurred between humanity and God. Adam and Eve were cast out from the Garden of Eden and humanity henceforth had to labor to survive. The search for food and water drove mankind to the various reaches of the earth. Generations went by and the world was soon inhabited and dominated by men. With the slow passing of time, consumed by their carnal impulses and their desire for power, humanity forgot the source of their origin, their God. Lost in the abyss of these pleasures, these idols, which they held above their own Creator, the vast majority of humanity had fallen into corruption and sin. Carelessness had overtaken them and they became blinded by their own indulgences.

There were, however, a few who had not forgotten the ways of the Lord God. Thus, we arrive at the story of Noah and his family (cf. Gn 6:5). Amidst the wickedness of the godless, Noah and his family found favor with God. God said to Noah, "I see that the end of all mortals has come, for the earth is full of lawlessness because of them. So I am going to destroy them with the earth" (Gn 6:13). He instructed Noah to build an ark[i] big enough to fit his family and two of every animal, male and female. At the appointed time, they boarded the ark and awaited God's judgment upon the earth.

The rains fell from the heavens and a flood enveloped the earth. Nothing except those within the ark survived. Once the flood had subsided, the ark safely made landfall as the waters dissipated. God commanded Noah and his family, as he did with Adam and Eve, to be fruitful and multiply and to fill the earth (cf. Gn 9:1). Never again would such a flood consume the earth, and as a symbol of this promise, God gave Noah a sign – a bow in the sky (i.e. a rainbow). This was the first covenant (post-Fall) to be established between God

---

[i] *Arca* in Latin, meaning box.

and humanity. This covenant, or pact, was made between God and all of creation. This would not be the last time God intervenes in the affairs of mortal men. The comforts of the earth can easily distort the memories and lessons of the past. As we shall soon see, God must once again reach out to humanity and establish yet another covenant.

Before we enter into the next biblical account, I find it important to first discuss the origin and meaning behind this story. As noted before, the most important thing to draw from these stories are the truths that they convey. This particular story of the Flood shares a commonality with several Babylonian stories of a flood indicating that these stories may have been drawn from the same source. This indicates that there may have been a flood(s) that occurred in the region of the Euphrates and Tigris. The biblical account expands beyond this region and applies it to the rest of the earth to convey an eternal truth, namely, that God is just and merciful to those who remain faithful even amidst the perversity of human behavior. Finally this story pre-figures the saving waters of baptism, which we will later discuss when we arrive at the sacraments.

As always, with the passing of time, people once again forget God's saving act. It seems people always forget about God when things tend to go well. The Bible provides an account for why we have many languages and nations on earth. Like the stories that precede it, this one too conveys an important lesson. We arrive at the Tower of Babel. The word *babel* as used in this particular context means "to confuse." The name, however, actually means "gate of god" according to the Babylonians. With this understanding of the word, the meaning of the story and the truth it is trying to convey becomes clearer.

As the story goes, humanity was united as one, not in faith, but in ambition, and they decided to build a city and a tower to make a name for themselves. They were united under one language with the same vocabulary. Their goal was to build a tower that would reach heaven, "the gate of God." God saw their pride and decided to confuse their language to where they could no longer understand each other. In their confusion, they abandoned their plans to finish the tower and they dispersed from each other. This story portrays the evils of secularism. Similar to Adam and Eve, rather than receiving God's grace they sought to steal it for themselves. Secularism seeks to unite humanity not in faith but in worldly matters. This way of thinking seeks to diminish the spiritual, glorify the material, and idolize the individual. Humanity can only be fully united under the banner of heaven. This biblical story not only provides an explanation for the rise of nations, but more importantly it conveys the truth and evils of secularism, an evil that is all too relevant today.

This brings us to God's second covenant. From among the nations, God chose a man called Abram (later named Abraham) to make his covenant. Putting faith in God, Abraham and his wife leave their country and kin to an unknown land. Abraham and his wife were barren and he wanted a child more than anything in the world. For a married couple, I cannot imagine anything more painful than the bleak reality of being unable to have your own children. But for God nothing is impossible. In fact there seems to be a recurring trend throughout the Bible of miraculous births. Hearing Abraham's prayer, God took Abraham outside and told him: "Look up at the sky and count the stars, if you can. Just so, he added, will your descendants be" (Gn 15:5). Thus, God made a covenant with Abraham that from his line a new people would arise: the people of Israel. Yet, because they were impatient, Abraham's wife, Sarai (later named Sarah), who had been unable to produce an offspring, suggested to Abraham to take her slave girl and sleep with her. Abraham seems to have accepted her offer without giving it a second thought. The slave-girl, Hagar, conceived from Abraham a son. Sarai became jealous and began to hold Hagar in contempt. This put Abraham in a bad spot. Unable to decide what to do, he told Sarai to treat Hagar as she pleased. Sarai treated Hagar so badly that she ran away.

To put things in perspective, Abraham and Sarai wanted a child of their own, but rather than allowing God to fulfill his promise at his appointed time, they decided to fulfill the promise themselves. A valuable lesson is learned here: nothing will go right if we force God's hand. Because of their actions, they created a feud amongst themselves and left a poor innocent slave-girl named Hagar at the mercy of their anger. God, seeing all this unfold, took pity on Hagar and made her a promise, that if she returned to Abraham and Sarai, he would bless her with descendants as numerous as Abraham's. God told her that when the child is born, he is to be named Ishmael, which means, "God listens," because he has heard her cries. The Muslims hold the tradition that this is where their ancestors came from – from the son of Hagar. Amidst the warfare that has plagued Muslims and Christians throughout the past centuries, it seems we have forgotten the commonality we share in our ancestral heritage. Yes, it is true – we are related, but when we make decisions on our own, in God's absence, there will always be division and quarrel among ourselves. It is no different today as it was in the past.

As promised, however, God did give Abraham and Sarah a son even in their old age. They named him Isaac. As a sign of God's covenant, Abraham along with his son, Isaac, and every male of his kin, was circumcised. This was the outward sign that marked the descendants of Abraham as the chosen people of God. To test his loyalty, however, God decided to put Abraham to the test. He asked of Abraham the unthinkable: to sacrifice Isaac as a burnt offering. That's right, God asked Abraham to offer up his only true heir, the same son God had promised him when he made the covenant. Imagine what went through Abraham's mind. Oblivious to what was going on, Abraham's son, Isaac, did exactly what his father told him to do and collected the wood for the sacrifice. He thought they were going to sacrifice a sheep. He became suspicious, however, when he noticed his father did not bring a sheep with him. When he asked about the sheep, Abraham replied: "My son, God himself will provide the sheep for the burnt offering" (Gn 22:8). Trusting in his father, Isaac went along with what Abraham told him. After they had built an altar for the sacrifice, Abraham bound his son and put him on the altar. He took his knife, and right before he was going to bring it down on his own son, an angel of the Lord stopped him and said: "Do not do the least thing to him. For now I know that you fear God, since you did not withhold from me your son, your only one" (Gn 22:12). Abraham passed the test.

Why would God impose such a difficult demand on Abraham? Did God really intend Abraham to sacrifice his own son? The answer regarding God's intent lies in the outcome. It was God's intention to have Abraham definitively display his trust, especially after he took on Hagar to bear him a son instead of trusting in God's appointed time. Based upon the angel's intervention, we can conclude that God had never intended for any harm to befall Isaac. In fact, God himself knows what it feels like to have a son sacrificed, as we will later see.

Eventually Abraham's descendants, the Hebrews, end up in Egypt. How they got there is a long story. We will skip that part of the story and go straight to Moses.

By the time Moses was born the Hebrew people have been undergoing extreme persecution by the Egyptians. As their numbers grew in Egypt, pharaoh began to see them as a threat to his empire. He had the Hebrew people enslaved, and he murdered all the newly born males by throwing them into the Nile River. One, however, was spared from pharaoh's wrath. This baby would grow up to be the most important person in Judaism as well as the most important person in the Old Testament. I, of course, am talking about Moses. In the midst of the persecutions, his mother, in desperation, put her son in a basket and let it float down the Nile River. Her daughter followed the basket from a distance to see who would discover it. As fate would have it, the basket was discovered by none other than the pharaoh's daughter who was bathing in the river. Because the baby was drawn from the water, he was given the name "Moses," which in Hebrew means "to be drawn out." Although this is a popular interpretation of how Moses received his name, chances are that pharaoh's daughter did not speak Hebrew and instead the name derived from the shortened Egyptian word *Tutmoses*, which means "the god Tut is born."[3]

Moses grew up within the Egyptian household and was treated like one of their own. When Moses was already a grown man, he witnessed an Egyptian slave-driver beat a fellow Hebrew. When he saw that no one was watching he killed the Egyptian and buried his body in the sand. He became afraid when word began to spread of his crime and before pharaoh could capture him he ran away into the desert. He came to a settlement whose leader was a Midianite priest. He was welcomed into the family and Moses married the priest's daughter.

As the years went by, the pharaoh of Egypt died and his son took over. The Hebrew people cried to God because they suffered greatly at the hands of the Egyptians. God heard their cries and remembered the covenant he made with Abraham. Little did Moses know that he would be the one chosen by God to go back to Egypt and free his people. As the story goes, God appeared to Moses in the form of a burning bush that could not be consumed by its flames. When Moses asked whom it was that was speaking to him, God replied by saying, "I am who I am (Ex 3:14)," which abbreviated is YHWH. God wanted Moses to return to Egypt and free the Hebrews, and though he did not want to go, he was finally persuaded and did as God commanded. To make a long story short, with the help of a lot of miraculous works, Moses was able to free the people of Israel from the tyranny of Egypt. The following events would shape Judaism forever. Moses brought the people before Mt. Sinai (also known as Mt. Horeb) to speak with God. In sacred scripture, it was quite common for an individual to communicate with God from a point of great elevation, such as a mountain, because it made them feel physically closer to God. From the top of Mt. Sinai, Moses receives from God the Ten Commandments (cf. Ex 20:3 & Dt 5:7). Here is a good time to pause and discuss them.

The first three commandments deal with humanity's relationship with God. The last seven deal with how humanity treats each other.

1ˢᵗ Commandment: You shall not make for yourselves a carved image. What does this mean? During the time that this commandment was given, many of the Hebrew people believed in various superstitions and that there were more than one God. One of these gods they believed was Ba'al, the god of fertility. This commandment sought to redirect their focus to the one true

God — the God of their fathers, Abraham and Isaac, by which God had established his covenant. As I mentioned before, many of the Israelites believed in other gods and they would literally "carve" images of these deities. These carvings or moldings are called "idols." An idol is anything worshiped above God. There are many of these idols that exist today. For example, money is an idol that is commonly "worshipped" above God. Some people would rather devote all their time to their job(s) instead of fulfilling their obligations to God. Notice I used the word "devote" from the word "devotion." Devotion is closely related to worship because it involves a committed love or a religious fervor towards something. The idol, I would say, that dominates today's society is the idol of the "self" or self-worshipping. This idol is directly related with the sin of pride and draws all attention to the self. This occurs when we place ourselves before everything. This idol manifests itself predominantly through self-gratification. This explains the decline in marriages, Mass attendance, abortions, pornography, atheism and agnosticism — all of which draws attention to the self and disregards the dignity of others (not to mention one's own dignity). More than anything else, idols draw us away from God, whom we should place above everything else: "No one can serve two masters. He will either hate one and love the other, or be devoted to one and despise the other" (Mt 6:24).

2nd Commandment: You shall not take the name of the Lord your God in vain.

The historical context of this commandment involves the ancient practice of oath taking. More solemn oaths invoked a deity to be the witness and judge of the oath's veracity. To invoke YHWH to witness and judge a false oath would be to "take the name of YHWH your God in vain." For us today, this commandment does not only imply that we should keep from invoking God's name during a false swearing (e.g. "I swear to God that my dog ate my homework"), but also when used in a profanity. This commandment also applies any

15

time we use God to accomplish our own agendas. For example, if I said something such as, "God wants you to give me all your money," it would be a manipulative way of using God for my own benefit.

3rd Commandment: You shall honor the Sabbath. For the Jews, the Sabbath is Saturday because it was the day God rested after creation. They in turn must also rest in thanksgiving for the fact that God gave us life. Christians also honor the Sabbath, but our day of rest is Sunday instead of Saturday. That is because through Christ's death and Resurrection we were given life anew, free from sin. Not only did Christ forgive us of our sins, but he also gave us eternal life. To remember and honor this, we go to Church on Sundays (the day Jesus rose from the dead). Therefore, it is our duty as Christians to go to Church every Sunday (or Saturday vigil). For many, too often this commandment is seen as a burden or an inconvenience to more "apparent" needs. This is usually a sign that the first commandment is already being compromised.

4th Commandment: Honor your father and mother. This means we must obey, respect, and care for our parents. As children, this means we must obey them and as adults we must look after them, especially in their late years. More often than not, parents are abandoned in nursing homes because it is an inconvenience for their children to look after. How easily they forget that they too will reach old age one day.

5th Commandment: You shall not kill (murder). This refers to unjustifiable killing. In other words, the killing of the innocent. Though killing another person is always an intrinsic evil, there are times where taking a life is justifiable such as in cases of a justifiable war, which seeks to safeguard or promote freedom and protect life. This is appropriately named a "just war." War should be a last resort because even though there are those who wish to harm us, they are still children of God. Legitimate self-defense, to protect one's life or one's loved ones, is also justifiable in cases where there is no other alternative. This commandment seeks to safeguard all life whenever possible.

6th Commandment: You shall not commit adultery. This commandment does not only refer to married couples but any individual who engages in the sexual act outside the sacrament of marriage. This is because when a sexual act is engaged outside of marriage, the individual is robbing the other of their future spouse's right to their body even if that future spouse is the one committing the act. Not only does the person rob the other of their body, but it also shows a lack of commitment since they are unwilling to make the relationship binding, which requires sacrifice, a sacrifice they are not willing to commit.

7th Commandment: You shall not steal. This also refers to instances where a party is denied proper compensation for legitimate services or products rendered. Property is an external expression of one's freedom, and to steal property from an individual is to compromise their dignity and freedom.

8th Commandment: You shall not bear false witness. In short, this means we should not lie. The way this commandment is phrased harkens to a courtroom setting. When a witness is called to a stand they are not to bear "false witness" to what they have seen. The truth is a good. There are rare cases, however, where a higher good may take precedence over a lower good, such as in cases where life is at stake. For example, during Hitler's reign over Europe, the Vatican disguised hundreds of Jews as Catholic priests to keep them from being transported to concentration camps. This principle is called "The Principle of Double Effect." The moral action of withholding the truth must have the certitude of a positive outcome without the direct intention of causing evil. It is never permissible to use evil means for a positive outcome.

9th Commandment: You shall not covet your neighbor's wife. This commandment is related to the sixth commandment. This commandment is intended to keep us from desiring other people's spouses. This includes the viewing of pornography, which undermines the dignity of those exposed. Originally, when this commandment was given to the Hebrews, women were viewed as property, and to take someone else's wife was equivalent to theft.

10th Commandment: You shall not covet your neighbor's goods. This means we must not be jealous of what others have. This sin can be tied with the sin of greed (a mortal (Capital) sin).

While Moses was atop of the mountain receiving the commandments from God, the people of Israel began to forget what God did for them, i.e. freeing them from slavery. Without the leadership of Moses, they began to turn to foreign gods. They asked Moses' brother, Aaron, for permission to build an idol of the god Ba'al to worship. Ba'al was the ancient god of stormclouds, fertility and agriculture. To appease the people, Aaron reluctantly agreed to let them build the idol, which was made from the gold of their jewelry. The idol, or statue, was in the form of a bull (or calf), the symbol of the god Ba'al. God saw what was taking place and told Moses that he would destroy the people for what they have done, but Moses reminded God of the covenant he made with Abraham and his anger abated. When Moses finally descended from the mountain, he saw what the Israelite people were doing, and in his rage he threw down the tablets upon which the Ten Commandments were written. Moses took the idol they made and melted it in a fire, which he then grounded to a powder. He then made the rebellious Israelites drink the powder (cf. Ex 32:20). He then said to the people of Israel, "Whoever is for the Lord, come to me!" (Ex 32:26). Those from the tribe of Levi all joined Moses. The rest were slain. 3,000 Israelites fell that day. Because of their disobedience, the Israelites were made to wonder in the desert for 40 years until that corrupted generation finally died off. Only the next generation was considered worthy to enter into the Promised Land.

Moses himself never made it to the Promised Land. It is said he was denied entrance because of an incident in which he lacked faith. As the story goes, as the Israelites were wondering in the desert, they grew thirsty and God commanded Moses to speak to a rock to yield water. The bickering of the people upset Moses to the point where he said to them, "Just listen, you rebels! Are we to produce water for you out of this rock?" and he struck the rock twice with his rod (staff) and the water flowed out abundantly. It is said that Moses' lack of faith was due in part because he struck the rock rather than speaking to it, like God commanded, and he and Aaron took credit for the miracle instead of giving it to God. Remember, they said, "are we," as in Moses and Aaron, "to produce water," instead of saying "shall God produce water for you from this rock?" Finally his lack of faith is further manifested by the fact that he had to strike the rock twice instead of once. Many believe this is what caused Moses and Aaron to be denied entrance into the Promised Land.

Instead, Joshua was the one chosen to lead the people of Israel into the Promised Land. The name "Joshua," in fact, means "savior." The name "Jesus" also derives from the name "Joshua." Through conquests of the neighboring tribes, such as the Hittites, Canaanites, Moabites, Philistines and others, Joshua was able to finally acquire the Promised Land with God's help. As long as the people of Israel put their trust in God they would continue to win every battle. This brings us to the establishment of the Kingdom of Israel. The Israelites wanted a king for themselves like the neighboring kingdoms. Up until then, judges appointed by God, like Samuel for instance, ruled over them. The reason God did not want them to have a king was precisely because he did not want Israel to be like the other nations and because a king was likely to pass the governance of the people down to his sons, rather than individuals chosen by God. This also meant that an individual would *directly* be ruling over the people of God rather than God himself. Nevertheless, the Israelites appointed a man named "Saul" to be their king. Samuel had warned the Israelites of the problems that would come from having a king. He warned that they would be made servants of the king rather than servants of God, and secondly, a king would likely try to maintain his power and keep it within his family (which is exactly what Saul tries to do).

David & Solomon

Saul turns out to be a poor leader who makes poor decisions and eventually rebels against God. During this same time, a young boy by the name of David begins to be a household name. David, a shepherd boy, slays Goliath, a Philistine of enormous size and reputation. As the story goes, Goliath challenges to fight against Israel's best soldier for dominance. Everyone feared Goliath and no one dared to challenge him. David, guided by God, takes up the challenge. Goliath said to David: "Come here to me, and I will feed your flesh to the birds of the air and the beasts of the field." (1 Sam 17:44). David, unflinching, said: "You come against me with sword and spear and scimitar, but I come against you in the name of the Lord of hosts, the God of the armies of Israel whom you have insulted. Today the Lord shall deliver you into my hand; I will strike you down and cut off your head. This very day I will feed your dead body and the dead bodies of the Philistine army to the birds of the air and the beasts of the field; thus the whole land shall learn that Israel has a God. All this multitude, too, shall learn that it is not by sword or spear that the Lord saves. For the battle belongs to the Lord, who shall deliver you into our hands" (1 Sam 17:45–47). Using his sling, he strikes Goliath on the forehead with a stone and kills him instantly. He grabs Goliath's own sword and uses it to cut off his head. This story once again shows that for God nothing is impossible.

The people of Israel loved David and Saul immediately became jealous. Saul sought to kill David but he was able to elude the various assassination attempts. When obsession for power consumes a person they tend to make enemies of many. Saul had no intention of giving up his power and his jealousy would make him an enemy of God. Many of God's priests sided with David and Saul had ordered his men to kill them all, but his men would not dare touch the priests of the Lord (cf. 1 Sam 22:17). One of his men by the name of Do'eg, however, carried out the order and killed over 80 of God's priests including all the women, children and livestock in the town of Nob.

David had two opportunities to kill Saul but he spared his life both times because he was righteous and he recognized Saul as God's anointed king, even though he had made himself an enemy of God. Even after being spared by David twice, Saul continued to pursue him. David found refuge with the Philistines, and he befriended one of their kings. The king offered David and his 600 men safety and a place to stay. During this time, Saul was still waging war against the Philistines, but David kept away from the conflict. Saul was eventually overpowered by the Philistines and rather than being captured, he fell upon his own spear. He was still alive, however, when the Philistines found him and he called over to one of them and begged him for death. The Philistine obliged and cut off his head. This very same man appeared to David three days later and reported to him what had happened. David became upset because he had killed Saul, God's anointed king. Even though Saul and David were enemies, they were still both sons of the house of Israel. Because of this, David had Saul's killer slain. Not only had Saul died, but Jonathan, his son, and David's closest friend, was also killed during the battle. David wept for both of them. Henceforth, David would become known as the greatest king of Israel.

It's not to say that David was without faults either. While looking out from the royal palace, he was able to see a woman bathing who just happened to be very beautiful. Her name was Bathsheba. David immediately fell head-over-heels and he greatly desired her. The problem was she happened to be married to a Hittite by the name of Uriah who served in David's army. He took her into the royal palace and slept with her anyway. There is much speculation whether David was solely at fault here. For example, what was Bathsheba doing bathing outside exactly when David just happened to be walking upon the palace roof? Some speculate she knew exactly when David strolled about the palace roof and she purposely sought to catch his attention. As it turned out, David impregnated her and he feared his adulterous act would be exposed. He sent her back to her husband hoping he would sleep with her in hopes of pinning the pregnancy on him, thus, covering up the adultery. Unfortunately for David, Israel was still waging war against neighboring kingdoms and under Mosaic Law soldiers were not allowed to engage in sex prior to a battle. As much as David wanted Uriah to sleep with his wife, being faithful to the laws of Israel though he himself was a Hittite, he would do no such thing. This led David to commit his greatest sin: he commanded Uriah's officers to place him in the front lines, and when the battle became intense, they were to pull back leaving Uriah completely exposed and defenseless. Uriah did not stand a chance, and as David wanted, Uriah was killed in the battle leaving his wife a widow. With Uriah gone, David married Bathsheba. God became angry with David for what he had done. Although David was able to keep his actions a secret, nothing can be kept secret from God. Nathan, a prophet and counselor to King David, was sent by God to confront David regarding his sinful deed. When David found out that God was angry with him, he became distressed and asked for forgiveness. Though God would eventually forgive David, his sin would not go unpunished. Because of his evil deed, David's unborn son would not live beyond birth. David became angry with himself for having offended God that he publicly asked forgiveness. He even danced naked through the streets of Jerusalem to show his humility and remorse. Imagine seeing your nation's leader dancing naked before the world! As was told to him, David's first son died upon birth, but seeing David's penitent heart, God forgave him and granted him another son with Bathsheba by the name of Solomon. Solomon would become Israel's last great king, for soon after, the kingdom would fall into the hands of, shall we say, unworthy, or rather, incompetent kings.

Solomon was known for many things: his wisdom, the Temple, and his many wives. David had planned to build a temple in Jerusalem but he died before the plans were carried out. Solomon not only built the Temple, but it was said to be one of the greatest structures of his time. When Herod was king during the time of Jesus, his Second Temple expansion was said to be one of the great wonders of the world, but we'll discuss that later. The Temple made Jerusalem the center of worship for the kingdom, and all sacrifices had to be done within the Temple itself. Before its construction, worship and sacrifices were done in various shrines throughout the kingdom. By having sacrifices in Jerusalem, the kingdom became more united and emphasized the importance of Jerusalem as its capitol. Many people made pilgrimages to the Temple to have their sins expiated through Temple sacrifices. This was done by following the mosaic law of killing an animal as an offering to God. These animals included goats, rams, lambs, doves, cows and bulls. These animals shed their blood as substitutes for the sinner. In other words, these animals would acquire the sins of the sinner and sacrificed on behalf of the penitent. This is important to know in order to understand Jesus' title as the Lamb of God.

The Temple was one of Solomon's greatest achievements, but he is also equally known for the wisdom God gave him. As the story goes, God told Solomon he would grant him anything he desired, but instead of asking for money or power, Solomon asked for wisdom to govern his people. God, moved by Solomon's request, granted him the wisdom he desired. Solomon exercised this wisdom when two women claiming to be the mother of a child confronted him. Solomon was to decide which mother was the real one. He came up with a clever way to find out to whom the child belonged. He told both women that he would cut the baby in half so that each could have an equal share of the baby. The real mother was so overcome with fear that the king would harm her baby that she immediately told Solomon that she would rather give her child to the other woman than to see the child die. It was then that Solomon realized who the real mother was and he handed the baby over to her (cf. 1 Kgs 3:16–28).

Solomon's wisdom made him a great diplomatic leader and he was able to bring peace to the Kingdom of Israel. Eventually, however, his wisdom ironically became his downfall. He became so arrogant with his wisdom that he began to neglect God and his teachings. He began marrying women from various kingdoms as a way of strengthening political ties. These women perverted him with strange teachings and strange religions. Foreign gods were welcomed from the surrounding cultures, which divided the worship of the One True God. Solomon's heart and that of many of the Israelites became divided. Solomon would go on to marry an astonishing 700 wives and 300 concubines (cf. 1 Kgs 11:3). It was clear that Solomon allowed himself to be overcome by insatiable lust and his desire for power, and this once great servant of God who was regarded in such high esteem had now fallen into the deceptive allurements of a false joy. Today, that false joy continues to be the pleasures of this world, which distracts us from the source of *true* joy, and only leads to a greater appetite for that which we intrinsically long for. Just as Solomon allowed his own wisdom (or rather false wisdom) to impede him from loving God, we too impede ourselves by replacing God with our venture for worldly pleasures and the idolization of our scientific conquests. Science is supposed to lead us to a greater understanding of God by unveiling the complexities of His creation so that we may understand and marvel at his great works. Instead, we use science as a means of halting human wonder and contemplation. We seem to have this obsession with objectifying everything around us – including ourselves. We fail to acknowledge the mystery of our being and the beings around us. When was the last time we contemplated the beauty of a sunset, or the miracle of a birth? Have we really turned everything around us into objects? Have we really degraded ourselves into believing that we exist only to be on the receiving end of stimuli? If so, we have made life meaningless and void.

After Solomon had died the kingdom quickly split in two: the north became the Kingdom of Israel (ten tribes), the south became Judah (two tribes). The capital of the north became Samaria. The capital of the south remained Jerusalem. Tensions arose between the two kingdoms. These tensions would resonate even through the time of Jesus. With Israel divided, it made it easier for neighboring civilizations to attack and conquer the Hebrews. First were the Assyrians, followed by the Babylonians. The object of their conquests was not Israel, but rather the wealth of Egypt. Israel just happened to be in the way. The Assyrians massacred and committed unspeakable crimes against the Israelites. Babylon came in and vanquished Assyria, but they in turn captured and exiled the Israelites from their lands. Not only did they enslave the Hebrews, but they also pillaged and destroyed the Temple. For the people of Israel, this was the greatest abomination because this meant they could no longer perform sacrifices for the remission of their sins.

During their exile, the Israelites questioned the cause of their departure from the Promised Land. They came to the conclusion that it was because they neglected and disobeyed God's commandments. This is clearly seen in the redactions[i] they made to their sacred writings. They also blamed Solomon for meddling in the affairs (no pun intended) of other nations rather than having their nation rely on God alone. Many chose not to marry foreign women so as not to be led astray from the faith. Some, however, did marry foreign women and never returned to their native land. Eventually, the Babylonians were conquered by the Persians, and they in turn were conquered by the Greeks. When the Persians came into power, the Hebrews were freed from their captivity and allowed to return to their lands. Many chose not to return. Those that did had to start anew. They rebuilt the Temple but it was merely a shadow of its former self. With the passing of time, the liturgy became more refined and great focus was placed on following the commandments, including the over 600 mosaic laws, so as to avoid another exile. They believed the first exile was a direct result of their disobedience to God, which would explain why God lifted his protection. Although they were allowed to return to their land and govern themselves, they were not, however, free from the sovereignty of the Persians. When the Greeks conquered the Persians, they in turn became the new sovereign. It was only a matter of time before Rome would step in and become the supreme ruler of the known western world.

---

[i] A re-editing or addition to a text by a different author. An example of an addition would be 1 Kgs 9:6–9 and Dt 29:23–28, which explicitly explains why the Temple was destroyed and the people are in exile. This is a clear example of an author interjecting his views to explain his current situation in exile by adding to a past story.

The Messiah

With Rome in place as the new world super power, the Western world becomes united under one language, one governance, and one ruler: Caesar. Ironically enough that shared language is Greek, (specifically *koine* Greek, meaning "common Greek") adopted from Alexander the Great, which he put in place during his conquests. Not only were they united in language, but also in road systems, trade routes and even in Greek culture (often called *Hellenism*). These factors paved the way for the coming of the Son of God and the spread of Christianity. Jesus could not have come at a more perfect time to proclaim the gospel.

Before we discuss who Jesus is and his role in the Trinity, we must first take a pause from our narrative and discuss the state of the Jewish people and the expectations they had of their anticipated "messiah," or "anointed one."[4] The anointed one (*Christus* in Latin and *Christos* in Greek) was believed to be the one who would have the Spirit of the Lord: "The spirit of wisdom and understanding, spirit of counsel and might, the spirit of knowledge and the fear of the Lord" (Is 11:2). The question is, "what must the messiah do?" This question will be the basis for Jesus' own temptations, as we will later see. The messianic promises, as these expectations are called, come in a variation of the following:

1) **The Zealot Approach:** An earthly Jerusalem, independent from foreign rule, acquired through force and led by a conqueror sent by God (like in the days of King David).
2) **The Judas Iscariot Approach:** An independent earthly Jerusalem acquired through peace led by God's anointed one.
3) **The Suffering Servant Approach:** One who would suffer and be put to death for the sins of humanity, as foretold in the Suffering Servant passages of Isaiah, which would bring about a "New Jerusalem," a new kingdom.

The first two are about power and glory, but the third leads to suffering for a much greater prize: what was once lost in the Garden of Eden (a Heavenly Jerusalem). Many would be influenced by these messianic promises, from King Herod to Jesus' own apostles.[5] We will discuss this more in depth later.

Not only had the surrounding culture and politics of the time impact Jewish society, but liturgy and worship had also evolved since the construction of the Second Temple (around 538-515 B.C.). By the time we arrive at the reign of Emperor Augustus Caesar (nephew of Julius Gaius Caesar), Judaism has divided itself into three principal groups: *Pharisees*, *Sadducees*, and *Essenes*.

The group that Jesus tends to run into most frequently is the Pharisees. They focused a lot on the Oral Tradition given to Moses at Mt. Horeb (Sinai), including the Written Law, or *Torah*. One aspect of the Pharisaic tradition that sets them apart from the Sadducees is their belief in an afterlife. They believed one's actions in his/her earthly life dictated whether one would be rewarded or punished in the afterlife. They also believed in the coming of a messiah, an "Anointed One," who would bring peace to Jerusalem. This expectation is very much in line with the second messianic promise I stated above.

The Sadducees were an elitist priestly group that focused on a strict, literal interpretation of the Written Law. This meant they had very little regards towards the prophets and rabbinical readings, like the Pharisees. Since the Written Law did not mention an afterlife, the Sadducees dismissed the notion of a resurrection. This belief led them to believe that if you followed strict obedience of the Torah you would be rewarded in the current life. This meant that if you are poor or sick it is because you had sinned or inherited the sins of your parents and are therefore suffering the consequences. Subsequently, because most of their practices centered on the Temple itself, it's no wonder why they disappeared after its destruction in 70 A.D.

Both the Pharisees and the Sadducees made up the *Sanhedrin*, a body of Jewish leaders that interpret the laws as well as oversee the civil livelihood of Judaic society. It was not uncommon for the members of the Sanhedrin to fall into dissention. A good example of this occurs in the Acts of the Apostles when Paul exploits the tension that existed between the two parties over the resurrection (cf. Acts 23:6).

The third group, the *Essenes*, were a group of people who were fed up with corruption and bureaucracy in the Temple and questioned the legitimacy of the Sadducean priesthood. They decided to separate themselves from the city of Jerusalem by living as a community in the desert with strict dietary laws. They focused on "purity of life" in anticipation of the messiah. Scholars believe the Essenes to be the inhabitants of Qumran from which were discovered the famous Dead Sea Scrolls. It is believed that this third group heavily influenced John the Baptist, who pointed his disciples to follow Jesus as the messiah. Archeological excavations show their living conditions may not have been the most sanitary considering their water supply did not come from a "flowing" source. Water that remains constant for long periods of time tends to build bacteria. Perhaps these difficult living conditions led to the site being abandoned.

Few actually believed the messiah had to die.[6] In fact, even Jesus' own followers did not expect Jesus to be crucified. To understand why Jesus had to suffer and die we must first take a look at who Jesus is as the Second Person of the Trinity and a closer look at the ramifications of The Fall, which could only be amended by a supreme divine act. Up until now, I have only mentioned God in the singular, as if he were one divine being, when in fact, God is three divine Persons. I did this for the sake of expressing a better understanding of Jewish theology, but we have come to the point in our story where the inner nature of God is slowly being unraveled through the revelation of Jesus the Christ.

We understand the Trinity indistinctly, "as in a mirror" (1 Cor 13:12), i.e. a blurry vision, because as human beings we can never fully comprehend the immensity of this mystery. It's almost like starring into the sun; we have trouble seeing it because it is too bright. Up until now we have been given bits and pieces of the whole in the Torah, the Sacred Writings, and the Prophets, but in the Second Person of the Trinity we begin to see the culmination of what has been already intricately woven thus far by revelation. A new dimension into the supreme and ultimate truth about ourselves and our relationship with God is made known in the person of Jesus. We now enter into the mystery of God himself as Three Persons.

In short, the Trinity is Love. The mission of Jesus Christ, the Son of God and Son of Man, can only be understood in the context of his relationship with his Father and his desire to amend what was broken between God and humanity. This, ultimately, was the Father's will. Israel's existence was the path by which God would come to all men.[7] Like the *Parable of the Tenants* (cf. Mt 21:33–41), after sending countless prophets, leaders, and judges, God the Father sends his own Son, knowing full well the price that would have to be paid for humanity's salvation. We will later discuss this "price" and why it had to be paid the way it was.

First we must understand the relationship between God the Father and God the Son, and the dynamic between the two. This "dynamic" is a mystery of extreme intimacy, which is very difficult to put into words. God the Father is the creator of all things and his very thoughts bring into being all things visible and invisible through his Word, the Son. In other words, the Father is life and he outpours his love unto all things. The Son, consubstantial with the Father (i.e. of the same essence), through his own eternal begetting, *is* the Father's love and offers it freely back to him. This intimacy epitomizes what love is, i.e. complete and radical self-giving. By its very nature, love is sacrificial. This exchange of love is life-giving and from it proceeds eternally the third person of the Trinity, the Holy Spirit. This exchange is called the *Trinitarian Economy* among theologians. The Trinitarian Economy, simply put, is the breathing in and breathing out of love. This "breath," so to speak, is the Holy Spirit, and the Holy Spirit gives life. Recall the creation of man, "God shaped man from the soil of the ground and blew the breadth of life into his nostrils, and man became a living being" (Genesis 2:7). God desires nothing more than to have us be a part of his infinite love. This can only happen if we are fully united with him, for this was God's plan from the very beginning.

The time had finally come for the Father to send his Son into the world: "Jesus has to enter into the drama of human existence, for that belongs to the core of his mission; he has to penetrate it completely, down to its uttermost depths, in order to find the 'lost sheep,' to bear it on his shoulders, and to bring it home."[8] Here is described one of the most famous quotes in all of scripture: "For God so loved the world that he gave his only Son, that whoever believes in him should not perish but have eternal life" (Jn 3:16). We have arrived at the most dramatic event in human history: The Incarnation, God becoming *in carne*, in the flesh. Jesus enters into our humanity to show us how to be fully human, and to be fully human is to imitate the love between the Father and his Son. We will be judged according to the way we imitate this love with one another. This gives us some insight into the mysterious meaning behind the title *Son of Man*: "The Son of Man is one person alone, and that person is Jesus. This identity shows us the way, shows us the criterion according to which our lives will one day be judged."[9]

For God to be fully man he had to be born of a woman. Not just any women, but the single most important human being in human history. From the beginning of time, God had chosen a special woman to be the vessel of his beloved Son. This woman was immaculately conceived,[i] i.e. born without Original Sin – the sin of our first parents. She is to be the New Eve, *woman* as she was created and meant to be, and her womb would be the New Eden, an intimate union with God once lost from humanity. Her name: Mary.

The Archangel Gabriel (lit. *Strength of God*), delivered to Mary the most important message ever received by humanity:

> Hail, favored one! The Lord is with you! ... Behold
> you will conceive in your womb and bear a son, and
> you shall name him Jesus [lit. *savior* from the Aramaic

---

[i] The question could be asked: "If Mary was conceived without original sin, then why can't all humanity be conceived without original sin? What is the necessity of an historic divine intervention?" The grace of her conception is predicated upon the future work of Christ, her son, and for the sake of His advent into the world. For God, Her conception and Christ's act is concurrent in God's "eternal now." But, Christ's work is still necessary.

Yesua]. He will be great and will be called Son of the Most High, and the Lord God will give him the throne of David his father, and he will rule over the house of Jacob forever, and of his kingdom there will be no end ... The Holy Spirit will come upon you, and the power of the Most High will overshadow you. Therefore the child to be born will be called holy, the Son of God (Lk 1:30–35).

Upon receiving the news that she would be the mother of the Son of God, Mary, in her humility, responds: "Behold, I am the handmaid of the Lord. May it be done to me according to your word" (Lk 1:38). Through her words and actions Mary becomes the model for all women, but I would be remiss if I did not mention her husband, Joseph, who becomes the model for all husbands and fathers. Jesus, thus, enters the world as man between the years 4-7 B.C., not 1 A.D., which was a miscalculation by Pope St. Gregory the Great's astronomers.

We have finally arrived at the Christ Event, but not everyone was ready for it. King Herod, for one, was familiar with the messianic promises and felt threatened that God's "Anointed One" would replace him as King of Judea. He immediately set out to eradicate the infant Jesus, though he didn't specifically know who he was. He did, however, know where he was to be born according to the prophecy that the Christ was to be born in the City of David, Bethlehem. He was not able to gain much information from the three wise men that were passing through in search of the newborn. Therefore, he decided to do something of unspeakable horror. The account of the Killing of the Innocents is only found in the Gospel of Luke, but considering Herod's nature as an established murderer (since he killed members of his own family including his wife), it is quite possible that Herod did kill every male newborn under the age of two in Bethlehem. Thanks to a dream Joseph had, the Holy Family escaped to Egypt, avoiding the onslaught. They would return to Galilee to Joseph's hometown of Nazareth after the death of King Herod, around the year 4 B.C.

The Apostles

Eventually the Holy Family returned to Nazareth where Jesus would grow up under the guidance of Mary and Joseph. From his early childhood he had a great love for the teachings of Sacred Scripture and he was often found in the synagogue and in the Temple among the teachers (cf. Lk 2:46), growing in wisdom and stature. Here the child Jesus shows us how we are to grow in favor with God and our fellow man, by studying and putting into the practice the teachings handed down to us. Not only would we grow in wisdom and understanding as Jesus did, but we would also grow in our love for God. As Mary kept everything Jesus did in her heart as he grew in love and understanding, so too will she keep us close to her heart if we obey the will of her Son.

To prepare the way for the messiah, John the Baptist, the son of Mary's cousin, Elizabeth, began preaching in the wilderness like, "a voice of one that cries in the desert" (Is 40:3), by baptizing with water those who sought repentance for their sins. Like the Essenes, John the Baptist was also fed up with the hypocrisy of the Pharisees and Sadducees, which may explain why he dwelt in the desert.

Before Jesus began his ministry, he asked John to baptize him in the river Jordan. John was unwilling at first because he did not feel worthy to baptize "the lamb of God that takes away the sin of the world" (Jn 1:29). Jesus persists by saying: "Leave it like this for the time being; it is fitting that we should, in this way, do all that uprightness demands" (Mt 3:15). What did Jesus mean by this? Did Jesus need forgiveness from sin? Quite the contrary. Jesus was baptized in the river Jordan for two main reasons: 1) to sanctify the waters of baptism so that henceforth, those who believed in him may be clothed in him through these same sanctifying waters and become a new creature in Christ (I will discuss this in greater detail when I discuss the Sacrament of Baptism); 2) and the second reason for Jesus' baptism is to reveal to the world that he is the Anointed Son of God. This is most evident by the words spoken by God the Father as the heavens opened and a dove (as symbol of the Holy Spirit) descended upon Jesus: "This is my beloved Son, with whom I am well pleased" (Mt 3:17). In a sense, the Baptism of Christ initiates or commissions his life of ministry. Similarly, Jesus is also revealed as the Son of God when he is "transfigured" before his apostles Peter, James and John, as a voice from heaven once again says, "this is my beloved Son," this time adding the words, "listen to him" (Lk 9:35), which is similar to the words of Mary, "do as he tells you" (Jn 2:5).

Here is a good time to introduce the apostles. Who were the apostles and why did they leave everything behind to follow Jesus? The apostles were a specific group of twelve men hand-picked by Jesus among his disciples to go forth and spread the Gospel, the Good News. The word *apostle* itself (*apostolos*) literally means, "one who is sent," like an ambassador. They were entrusted by Christ to carry out his teachings. Here we have the beginnings of the Church, whose primary purpose is to proclaim the teachings of Christ. In fact the teaching office of the Church is called the *Magisterium*, which comes from the Latin word *magister*, or "teacher."

The apostles came from distinctive backgrounds with equally distinctive ideas about the mission and attributes of God's "Anointed One." In order to understand what they did, why they did it, and why they said what they said, we must first understand what they expected from Jesus. Here, it is important to remember the messianic promises I mentioned earlier. Take Simon the zealot for example. The zealots were those that believed in the expectation of a messiah that would bring about an independent earthly Jerusalem even by force if necessary. Simon was part of this particular group and was most likely influenced by their ideas.

Some apostles and disciples believed in the expectation that Jesus would bring about an independent Jerusalem through peaceful means, such as Judas Iscariot, and at one point, most of the other apostles, including Simon Peter, James and even John.[10] The thought of Jesus suffering and being put to death was foreign to most of them.

For example, when Jesus told his apostles that he would suffer and be put to death upon entering Jerusalem, Simon Peter[11] rebuked him and said, "God forbid, Lord! This shall never happen to you!" (Mt 16:22), to which Jesus replied: "Get behind me Satan! You are a hindrance to me; for you are thinking not the way God thinks, but man" (Mt 16:23). In a different chapter, when Jesus reiterated his suffering and death, it once again went over their heads because James and John ignored the suffering and death part and asked Jesus if they could sit at his right and left when he reached his glory, (cf. Mk 10:37) or kingdom (cf. Mt. 20:20). Jesus responds saying, "Are you able to drink the cup that I am to drink?" (Mt. 20:22), meaning, can you suffer like I am to suffer? They both said yes, but when the time came, they all scattered. If they really could have drank the cup of suffering as they said they could, and stayed with him as he was arrested, then perhaps it would have been James and John crucified with Jesus instead of two thieves, thus fulfilling their desire to be at his right and left. Can *we* drink the cup that he drinks? Something to think about since we are all called to be *witnesses* of Christ, which is the literal translation of the word "martyr" (from the Greek *martur*).

No matter how many times Jesus foretold his suffering and death, Judas Iscariot was adamant about him fulfilling the expectation of bringing about an independent Jerusalem. Perhaps he thought Jesus was the peaceful solution to fulfilling this particular prophecy. This is why he wanted to plead his case to the Sanhedrin, the Jewish authorities, that Jesus was the true messiah. How easily he forgot the words spoken by Christ: "Do not think that I came to bring peace on the earth; I did not come to bring peace, but a sword. For I came to set a man against his father, and a daughter against her mother, and a daughter-in-law against her mother-in-law; and a man's enemies would be the members of his household" (Mt 10:34). Even today, we are able to see the divisions foretold by Christ as the separation between the faithful and the secular continues to grow and widen.

When Judas realized that he had betrayed Jesus, upon discovering the Sanhedrin's true intentions to kill him, he tried to return the thirty pieces of silver they gave him for revealing Jesus' location.

They would not take it back, and in his guilt, Judas committed suicide. Even Peter, himself, betrayed Jesus by denying him three times. The difference between Peter and Judas is that Peter repented and continued to follow Jesus even after his crucifixion.

Many people refused to believe that the messiah had to suffer. It's no surprise then why the masses chose Barabbas over Jesus; Barabbas was a freedom fighter, a zealot, who killed a Roman soldier to bring about an independent Jerusalem free from their Roman overlords. Even his name, *Bar-abbas*[12], literally meaning "son of the father," has a messianic ring to it. It's no wonder why many confused him for the messiah. They would rather see Jesus, the son of a carpenter, be crucified instead of Barabbas.

This is why we admire the apostles. Even amidst their doubts and persecutions they still followed Christ. We follow their teachings because even though they weren't perfect, they remained faithful to Jesus and did what he commanded them to do ... almost all unto death. This is what it means to be a saint. Are we willing to do the same?

The Sacraments

After his baptism, but before officially starting his ministry, Jesus went into the desert for forty days of intense fasting and prayer. During those forty days Satan (Hebrew for *adversary* or *the accuser*) tempted Jesus three times. I will take a closer look at the meaning of those temptations when I later discuss the nature of sin and ways to overcome it as I draw comparisons between Jesus' temptations and our own. I will say, however, that the temptations of Christ revolved around his mission and his identity as *Son of God*. Nevertheless, Jesus overcomes his temptations in the desert and begins his mission of proclaiming the Kingdom of God. During his mission, Jesus sets out not to abolish the law or the prophets but to fulfill them (cf. Mt 5:17). He not only builds upon the teachings of the Old Testament, but he makes them new so that we may grow closer to God and our neighbor. Along with this new teaching, he also gives us what are called *sacraments* so that we may faithfully adhere to said teachings and grow in holiness.

The sacraments are visible signs that keep us connected with Christ. They are of the spiritual realm but made visible in the physical realm so that they may be perceived by our senses, whether by touch, taste, smell, sight or hearing. They are efficacious by nature, meaning they work spiritual graces within us, transforming us closer to God. There are seven sacraments instituted by Christ: Baptism, Confirmation and Eucharist (called the *Sacraments of Christian Initiation*); Reconciliation and Anointing of the Sick (called the *Sacraments of Healing*); and Matrimony and Holy Orders (called the *Sacraments of Christian Service*).

Baptism

The first sacrament is Baptism. We cannot receive the other sacraments without first receiving Baptism because Baptism makes us sharers in the divine life and orders us towards worship as a community of believers. Baptism makes the person a Christian, a follower of Christ. Christ himself sanctified the waters in the Jordan, through his own baptism, to sanctify us in him. A number of graces occur in Baptism. Jesus, our savior, came to heal us from our sins. In Baptism, we are forgiven of all previous sins, including the sin inherited from our first parents, Adam and Eve, from which came The Fall (The Great Separation). Christ came to restore that union once lost in Paradise. With Christ, in accordance with his commandments, we can once again be united with him in Paradise. Like the crucified thief, we should all have the innate desire to hear these words spoken to us by Christ: "Truly I say to you, today you will be with me in Paradise" (cf. Lk 23:43).

In Baptism we are clothed in Christ, represented by the white garments worn during the ceremony as a symbol of our shared redemption in Christ. The waters of baptism remind us of the Great Flood that purified the earth during the time of Noah[i] as well as the floodwaters of the Red Sea, which saved the Israelites from the Egyptians. Like the Flood, the waters of Baptism purify us and free us from the slavery of sin (cf. 1 Pt 3:18-22). In Baptism we die in Christ and rise with him as a new creature, joining in his redemption as part of the New and Everlasting Covenant (cf. Rm 6:1-11). By being baptized, we undertake the Divine Command of going out "to the whole world" and "proclaiming the Gospel to all creation" (Mk 16:15). In baptism we become adopted sons and daughters of God the Father and we are united with Christ as his brothers and sisters, which makes us priests (to make sacrifice and offer right worship to God), prophets (to proclaim the Gospel) and kings (to share in God's kingship as his sons and daughters).

---

[i] There is even a connection made between the Great Flood and the Baptism of Jesus in the Jordon River by the appearance of a dove in Luke's gospel (cf. Lk 3:22).

Michael A. Garcia

Reconciliation & Anointing of the Sick

Even after our baptism, we are still inclined to sin because of our human nature (*concupiscence*)[i], which is why Jesus instituted the sacrament of Reconciliation, also known as Confession, and the sacrament of Anointing of the Sick. Both these sacraments bring healing and salvation. When we sin we sometimes do not know the full nature or implications that come with this or that particular "offense" in regards to our relationship with God, because as human beings, we are limited in understanding and we fail to see the extent we wrong God. It is not to say that we do not know when we commit evil, because it is necessary to know the act to be evil for it to be a sin. However, because of our lack of understanding, most people do not definitively choose to turn away from God. Ignorance is not a sin, but willfully choosing to remain in ignorance in fear that it might challenge us to change our lives, is. A *definitive* separation from God out of pure spite, which is voluntary, volitional, and bears full knowledge of its implications, is incapable of receiving pardon because the person, likewise, is incapable of asking for forgiveness so long as he or she remains obstinate. This sin against God himself is the sin of malice (*odium inimicitiae*), which is directly tied with the sin of pride. It is for this reason that the demons, because of the *kind* of knowledge they possess of God and His Will, can never ask for pardon, nor seek it.[13] This is often called the perturbation of angels.

Luckily most of us do not intentionally seek eternal separation from God when we sin. We will later discuss the different degrees of sin and the difference between vice and virtue, but for now

---

[i] "Although it is proper to each individual, original sin does not have the character of a personal fault in any of Adam's descendants. It is a deprivation of original holiness and justice, but human nature has not been totally corrupted: it is wounded in the natural powers proper to it, subject to ignorance, suffering and the dominion of death, and inclined to sin - an inclination to evil that is called concupiscence. Baptism, by imparting the life of Christ's grace, erases original sin and turns a man back towards God, but the consequences for nature, weakened and inclined to evil, persist in man and summon him to spiritual battle." *Catechism of the Catholic Church*, 2nd ed., 405.

we will concentrate on the sacrament itself. In the sacrament of Reconciliation we confess our sins to a priest, who is at that moment Christ himself. He is the mediator between God and humanity. Many ask, "Why must we confess our sins to a priest? Why can't we confess to God directly?" The answer lies in scripture itself. Before his ascension into heaven, Jesus himself gave authority to his apostles to forgive sins when he breathed the Holy Spirit on them and said: "Whose sins you forgive are forgiven them, and whose sins you retain are retained" (Jn 20:23). Remember that prior to this sins were only forgiven through the blood of an animal as a scapegoat. As the Lamb of God who sacrificed himself for our sins, Jesus establishes a new way for us to obtain forgiveness. Therefore, in the sacrament of reconciliation, priests fulfill Jesus' command to forgive the sins of those who are truly sorry, and retain the sins of those who are not. Thus, in the sacrament of reconciliation we become a clean slate, which recalls the cleansing waters of our baptism. Plus, nowhere in scripture – and that includes both the Old Testament and the New Testament – does it say that confessing your sins to God is a private occasion, so the argument that a person can confess their sins directly to God is actually anti-scriptural.

During moments of illness, the Church provides the sacrament of Anointing of the Sick, which like Confession, also removes sin. Every miracle that Jesus performed on a sick person pointed to a greater healing – a healing of the soul and an ease of the conscience. In Jesus' day, people believed they were born blind, or made a leper, or a paralytic because of some sin they or their parents had committed. Imagine being told your whole life that the reason you are sick is because of a shameful act that has now come to define who you are. Jesus, as the Divine Physician, healed both body and soul. By accompanying the physical miracle with the words, "your sins are forgiven," Jesus removes the shame that those poor individuals had to endure for all their lives. Similarly, Anointing of the Sick is forgiveness that initiates healing.[14] In his compassion for all those who are sick and suffering, Jesus tells his apostles to heal the sick (cf.

Lk 9:2), and the Church continues to follow that command through their successors.[i]

Holy Communion

The celebration of the Eucharist, in which we receive Holy Communion (the consecrated host known as *the Blessed Sacrament*), is the "source and summit of the Christian life"[15]. Although Baptism makes us Christians, and Confirmation makes us more configured to Christ, the Holy Eucharist completes Christian initiation[16]. In the Eucharist we are fully united with Christ because Christ himself is sacramentally present in body, blood, soul and divinity. The Eucharist is made present in the Mass as bread and wine are transformed into the Body and Blood of Jesus Christ. It is for this reason that the Mass[ii] is the most perfect expression of Christian liturgy. Jesus instituted this sacrament at his last supper when he said: "Do this in remembrance of me" (Lk 22:19). Jesus made it absolutely clear that, "unless you eat the flesh of the Son of Man and drink his blood, you have no life in you; he who eats my flesh and drinks my blood has eternal life, and I will raise him up at the last day" (Jn 6:53). The Israelites were fed in the desert with bread from heaven, but the bread Jesus offers, i.e. his own flesh, gives everlasting life. He is the true bread from heaven.

The Mass is literally the Last Supper made manifest again. The priest, in the person of Christ, becomes both priest and victim. The body of Jesus is once again broken and given to his disciples as a memorial of his death. As partakers of his body and blood we become intimately united

---

[i] See James 5:14

[ii] The *Mass*: "Before it became the technical name of the holy Liturgy in the Roman Rite, it meant simply 'dismissal'... So *Ite missa est* should be translated 'Go it is the dismissal'... The explanation is that originally the people were not dismissed on such days, but stayed in church for further prayers after Mass, suitable to fasting days."

Adrian Fortescue, "Ite Missa Est," *The Catholic Encyclopedia*, Vol. 8 (New York: Robert Appleton Company, 1910, Retrieved July 8, 2015), <http://www.newadvent.org/cathen/08253a.htm>.

with Christ himself, both in flesh and in spirit. This is Jesus' way of remaining in us. As he himself said: "I will not leave you as orphans; I will come to you" (Jn 14:18). It is for this reason that before one receives the Holy Eucharist, which literally means "thanksgiving," one should be disposed with a pure heart and approach with great reverence.

Too often many people receive the Eucharist immodestly and with an impure heart. It is for this reason that it is highly recommended to seek the Sacrament of Reconciliation prior to receiving Holy Communion, especially in cases of mortal sin. Recall Jesus' instruction before offering sacrifice to the altar: "So if you are offering your gift at the altar, and there remember that your brother has something against you, leave your gift there before the altar and go; first be reconciled to your brother, and then come and offer your gift" (Mt 5:24). In other words, leave all misdeeds, quarrels and sinful acts behind before approaching the altar of God. As St. Paul tells us: "Whoever, therefore, eats the bread or drinks the cup of the Lord in an unworthy manner will be guilty of profaning the body and blood of the Lord" (1 Cor 11:27).

The celebration of the Eucharist is many times described as the "Heavenly Banquet" and rightly so, for at that precise moment heaven and earth indeed meet. It is for this reason that after one has seriously considered the state of their spiritual being one should present themselves modestly in a way which does not detract attention from where attention is rightly due. Recall the parable of the wedding feast:

> And those servants went out into the streets and gathered all whom they found, both bad and good; so the wedding hall was filled with guests. But when the king came in to look at the guests, he saw there a man who had no wedding garment; and he said to him, 'Friend, how did you get in here without a wedding garment?' And he was speechless. Then the king said to the attendants, 'Bind him hand and foot, and cast him into the outer darkness; there men will weep and gnash their teeth' (Mt 22:10-13).

Although all are invited to the Heavenly Banquet, not all are properly or modestly disposed to receive the sacred Body and Blood of Jesus Christ. When I speak of modesty I am not simply referring to what someone wears, but more importantly, I am speaking of "spiritual modesty," i.e. to be clothed in humility. Through his sacrifice we have been privileged, not entitled, to receive this gift from heaven. Should we not, therefore, approach with the utmost reverence? We, as Catholics, are by our very nature a "Eucharistic people." Look at what J.R.R. Tolkien had to say about the Eucharist: "Out of the darkness of my life, so much frustrated, I put before you the one great thing to love on earth: the Blessed Sacrament. There you will find romance, glory, honour, fidelity, and the true way of all your loves upon earth..."[17]

Confirmation

The sacrament of Confirmation usually occurs before first Holy Communion for those adults who are being initiated into the faith, but for those who are already baptized Christians in the Latin Church, Confirmation usually follows after first Holy Communion. Although the Eucharist is the "Sacrament of sacraments,"[18] Confirmation strengthens the Christian in the Spirit. In fact, Confirmation completes the graces received in Baptism: "For 'by the sacrament of Confirmation, [the baptized] are more perfectly bound to the Church and are enriched with a special strength of the Holy Spirit. Hence they are, as true witnesses of Christ, more strictly obliged to spread and defend the faith by word and deed'"[19]. In other words, with the reception of Confirmation, we receive the title of "Defender of the Faith," which is no small title.

Confirmation fulfills Jesus' will of us being anointed in him by the Holy Spirit, which from the times of the Apostles, has always been associated with the laying-on of hands[20]. Jesus promised his disciples that those who seek him would be given the Father's seal (cf. Jn 6:27). As Paul the Apostle tells us, we were sealed with the Holy

Spirit for the sake of our redemption, as Jesus promised, because we believed in his message, the Gospel (cf. Eph 4:30; 1:13). Along with the laying of hands, sacred chrism is used to anoint the individual in Christ. In fact, the word *Christian* means "anointed" because we now share in the same Spirit that anointed Jesus[21]. With this mark, or seal, that the Holy Spirit gives us, we are granted seven gifts to strengthen our lives as Christians. These gifts are: the spirit of *wisdom* and *understanding*, the spirit of *right judgment* and *courage* (also referred to as *fortitude*), the spirit of *knowledge* and *reverence*, and the spirit of *holy fear* in God's presence, which helps us seek and recognize the good and avoid the evil[22]. These gifts grow every time a person does God's will, and they prepare us for the calling that God has in each and every one of us, whether it's the married life or consecrated life.

Matrimony

Here I would like to devote a great deal of time to the sacrament of matrimony because it is a sacrament that affects most Christians. In many ways, this sacrament is greatly misunderstood, partly because the surrounding culture gives us a false notion of what love really is. From the beginning of our humanity, man was never meant to be alone, as we have seen in Genesis. Sensing his loneliness, God took a part of Adam and made woman. Adam, enraptured by his love for Eve exclaims, "This is now bone of my bones and flesh of my flesh," and, "she shall be called woman," because she was taken from his side. Like Adam, the single desire that dominates our search for joy in life is to love and to be loved.[23]

What does this love entail? How does this love manifest itself? Real love is not a novelty, but rather a path that leads to authentic happiness.[24] This authentic love can only be fully expressed through total commitment and complete self-surrender. Husbands and wives give of themselves to each other, together with God, in complete union. In this way, they can avoid falling into the errors and miseries that occur when a heart is divided among the multiplicities of worldly pleasures.[25] This is an opportunity for couples to grow in a mature love that will allow them look upon each other with awe and wonder at the beauty and goodness found in the depths of their very beings. In this way, they can stand before each other (naked) like Adam and Eve and feel no shame (cf. Gn 2:25). When spouses look upon each other in this way they will come to know the difference between love's serenity and lust's darkness.[26] In practical terms, this means that married couples have the obligation and responsibility to protect each other from the language of those who boast and find praise in their lusts.[27] Couples must beware of falling into this trap, or they too may have to clothe themselves from each other's eyes (cf. Gn 3:21). Not only is this language not love, but it is also unnatural and contrary to God's will.[28] Instead, couples should embrace each other's beauty for its own sake – a "beauty seen not by the eye of the flesh, but only by inward discernment."[29]

In marriage, spouses are surrendering the rights of their own bodies to one another in a pronouncement that says, "I am yours and no other." Recall the words of St. Paul, "husbands ought to love their wives as their own bodies. He who loves his wife loves himself" (Eph 5:28). This is particularly true because a husband comes to know himself more fully through his wife. This is why it is the couple *themselves* who are the ministers at their wedding, not the priest or deacon officiating at the ceremony.

In marriage, couples are externalizing (making visible) what they have already made internally in the depths of their hearts. This is true sacrificial love. By contrast, those who undergo "trial marriages" (cohabitation prior to marriage) set themselves up for failure because they never surrender themselves fully such as in the binding contract of matrimony (we will speak more on that later). These people are willing to give up their bodies but not their hearts; they are of the flesh, but refuse to be joined as *one* flesh. In the sacrament of matrimony spouses are saying to one another, "I am prepared to spend the rest of my life with you to whatever end, for better or worse, because you are the love of my life, whom God has sent for me to share in this nuptial and sacramental union with." It is complete and total surrender without reservations.[30] This implies that the person is willing to give up the lifestyle they once had for the sake of the one they love.[31] It brings a person to set aside his or her own wants and desires for the sake of the other, and the fruit of such a commitment bears the blessing of a lifelong, joy-filled relationship which brings into being life itself.[32] "For this reason," Genesis tells us, "a man will leave his father and mother and be united to his wife, and the two will become one flesh" (Gn 2:24).

So what makes a Christian marriage different from a natural or civil marriage? Every human being has the natural right to marry. After all, God commanded it: "Be fruitful and multiply, and fill the earth and subdue it" (Gn 1:28). In a *natural* marriage, humanity as a whole may and can benefit if the individuals lead by example in the way they treat one another as ends in themselves.[33] In other words, they preserve each other's dignity by the mutual respect they have towards each other.[34] This, of course, seems like a reasonable approach, but a Christian, or *sacramental* marriage, not only elevates a natural marriage, but also gives it a new meaning. A sacramental marriage goes beyond the natural aspects of marriage and raises it to a supernatural level. In short, a sacramental marriage helps us to love to the full extent of our human capacity because we now desire to imitate the love that only God can give – sacrificial love. This changes everything because rather than entering into marriage for mutual satisfaction, the individuals become more concerned about the needs of the one they love rather than their own (both physically and spiritually).[35] Just as God the Father gives everything of himself to his Son, and he in return gives everything freely back to his Father, married couples are called to give everything of themselves to each other. Here, love is complete and ultimate.[36]

Is it any surprise then, that in John's Gospel we see something quite interesting? In fact, not just interesting but theologically significant. Jesus, God incarnate, performs his first miracle at a wedding banquet (cf. Jn 2:1-11).[i] The Son of Man and Son of God begins his ministry at a moment of intimacy. Christ, the Savior, shows us the path to holiness using spousal language. As I mentioned before, in marriage, spouses are to give of themselves completely without reservations. It constantly demands sacrificial love for the good of the spouses. This is made possible because the love between a husband and wife is so great they are willing to make themselves vulnerable to each other. Many times throughout the gospels Jesus refers to himself as "the bridegroom" and his purpose on earth is to show humanity how to be fully human. Here we have some more insight regarding Jesus' mysterious title "Son of Man." To be fully human is to fully love, and

---

[i] What is REALLY interesting is that the wedding at Cana is on the Seventh Day of John's allusion to Creation, and Jesus alludes to Mary as Eve...the restoration of Adam and Eve's marriage, as it were!

to fully love we must be sacrificial. The word "sacrifice" comes from the Latin, which literally means, "to make holy." Since we share the royal priesthood of Christ in Baptism, we are called to make these sacrifices each and every day of our lives, especially in the case of married couples, who offer their wants and desires in sacrifice daily. In so doing, they exercise their royal priesthood by living holy lives as witnesses of the Gospel, just as Jesus sacrificed himself without reservations for us.

This sacrificial love, upon which couples embark, is only possible through faith.[37] Only through faith can we understand why Jesus was sent by the Father and died for us. Only by believing in him can these words truly be applicable:

> May they all be one, just as, Father, you are in me and
> I am in you, so that the world may believe it was you
> who sent me. I have given them the glory you gave
> to me, that they may be one as we are one. With me
> in them and you in me, may they be so perfected in
> unity that the world will recognize that it was you
> who sent me and that you have loved them as you
> have loved me (Jn 17: 21-23).

That is why Christ is at the center of a sacramental marriage, because he is calling both spouses to be one in him as he is one with the Father, so that with Christ, the love they have for each other may be perfected. I strongly encourage couples to pray together and allow Christ to be at the center of their marriage. By allowing themselves to receive God's grace, they open themselves to a deeper and stronger faith, which in turn strengthens their marriage.

Often times, couples enter into marriage with an ideal, but this ideal may be putting unrealistic expectations on the other person. After all, the only perfect spouse is Jesus Christ. This is why communication is so important. Communication within a marriage should always include three persons: the husband, the wife, and Christ. At first, it may sound awkward to have a couple routinely pray together, but imagine the strength that can come from it. Imagine the strength that can come when a couple kneels together, even if for just two minutes before going to bed, and shares with God what they are thankful for, for any moments of happiness they've experienced, for any places that need healing, etc. Imagine the impact of having each of them hear their spouse verbalize to God how they desire to become a better person so that they may be a better husband or wife. This prayer time is not for couples to point out each other's faults, but a time to ask God to help them increase in virtue, beginning with the self. This is what it means to be in a "spiritual union." Only through faith can we hope to arrive at perfect love. In doing so, love points to what is eternal.[38]

Passion, Death & Resurrection

To fully grasp the sacrament of Holy Orders we must understand the mission of the One who instituted it, because essentially, the calling is one and the same; namely, giving up one's life, as Christ did, for the proclamation of the Gospel. This calling is directly tied with the mission entrusted by Christ to his apostles, i.e. to carry out the works of his Church. To understand what motivates these men to consecrate their very lives to Christ we must first return to our narrative and observe the One whom they seek to imitate.[39]

Jesus told his disciples that he had to enter into Jerusalem where, "the Son of Man will be handed over to the chief priests and the scribes, and they will condemn him to death and hand him over to the Gentiles who will mock him, spit upon him, scourge him, and put him to death, but after three days he will rise (Mk 10:33)." As I mentioned before, most, if not all, of his disciples could not fully grasp this reality. By this point, Judas himself had his own motives for Jesus. For him, as well as many others, Jesus was supposed to restore the kingdom of Israel to its former glory, as in the time of King David. We begin to see his denial of Jesus' true mission as early as the Eucharistic discourse of John 6:53 when Jesus tells his disciples that they must eat his flesh and drink his blood, which is connected to his suffering and death. When Jesus says at the Last Supper, "This is my body, which will be given for you (Lk 22:19)," he is referring to both the Eucharist and his death. The two are inseparable. It is precisely after Jesus tells his followers that they must eat his flesh that he discovered who would betray him because he saw that Judas did not believe (Jn 6:64). Woe to those who do not believe in the Real Presence of Jesus in the Eucharist!

At the Last Supper, when Jesus announced to his apostles that one of them was to betray him, they looked at each other and wondered who it would be. He let John and Peter know by handing a morsel of bread he had dipped in a dish to his betrayer. Upon doing so, he tells Judas, "What you are going to do, do it quickly" (Jn 13:27), referring to his betrayal. Judas was so intent on bringing about another Davidic kingdom that he mistook what Jesus had said and immediately went to the Sanhedrin to present his case that Jesus was indeed the messiah. Unfortunately for him, the Sanhedrin did not see things his way. They had plans of their own. Judas was so concerned with worldly power and glory that his heart was never opened to the reality of Jesus' true mission. By the time he discovered Jesus' true purpose it was too late; his betrayal was made known to him. Deeply regretting what he had done, he returned the thirty pieces of silver[i] to the chief priests and the members of the Sanhedrin, which he had received for revealing Jesus' location, but it was to no avail. They were so intent on killing Jesus by this point that nothing was going to stop their plans now. Judas exclaims, "I have sinned in betraying innocent blood," and flings the pieces of silver into the temple (Mt 27:4). It is then that he went and proceeded to hang himself. Judas revealed to us an important lesson: when we are so concerned with worldly matters, we close ourselves to spiritual ones, and in doing so, we bring upon our own death.

Before Jesus is arrested and taken to the Sanhedrin, we find him in the Garden of Gethsemane on the Mount of Olives. Jesus comes face to face with his impending suffering and death. Whereas the first Adam sought divinity for himself and brought upon his own death, the New Adam in complete submission to his Father, willingly offers himself up to death for the sake of all humanity. Even for Christ this was no easy task. Jesus shows humanity what greatness truly is by his suffering. As Paul tells us in his letter to the Hebrews, Jesus was tested in every way and yet he did not fall into sin (cf. Heb 4:15). Not only did Jesus show us the vulnerability of his humanity as his sweat fell to the ground as drops of blood, but he shows us what it means to be fully human: selfless. Jesus understands that he did not come to be served but to serve and to give his life as a ransom for many (cf. Mk 10:45).

---

[i] Similar to when Joseph was sold into slavery in Genesis 37:28.

In the garden of Gethsemane, the New Adam once again faces the temptation that has plagued his mission: avoidance of the cross. In his sorrow and distress, he falls to the ground and prays that this hour of agony may pass him by (cf. Mk 14:35). The anticipation of his death must have seemed unbearable for he reveals to us his human nature as he tells his Father, "Abba, Father, all things are possible to you. Take this cup away from me, but not what I will but what you will" (Mk 14:36). As he himself told Peter: "The spirit is willing, but the flesh is weak" (Mk 14:39). How often do we wish to do God's will but fall short because we too are weak in the flesh? It is during these difficult times that prayer is especially necessary. Eventually, Jesus perseveres in prayer and prevails, for he wishes to do nothing more than the will of his Father. Suffering is thus endured for those he loves. As Pope Benedict XVI tells us, "the constant temptation for Christians, indeed, for the Church," is, as he puts it, "to seek victory without the Cross."[40] There cannot be any victory without the cross.

Jesus is eventually brought before the Sanhedrin for trial. It soon becomes evident that they have no case against him, because not only did they present false evidence, but even their own witnesses could not seem to agree with each other's testimonies. It is not until Jesus answered the question posed by the high priest, Caiaphas, "Are you the Messiah, the son of the Blessed One?" that they finally condemn him. To that question, Jesus responded, "I am; and you shall see the Son of Man seated at the right hand of the Power and coming with the clouds of heaven" (Mk 14:62). To equate himself with the power of the great *I AM* was considered blasphemous to the Jews (recall that the name God revealed to Moses was "I am who I am").[41] Since the Jews could not put to death a person under Roman law, for Rome reserved that power to itself, they had to approach the Roman governor of that region, Pontius Pilate, to carry out the sentence.

I am not going to discuss the entire episode of Jesus before Pilate; however, I would like to point out one significant moment. During Pilate's conversation with Jesus, Jesus plainly tells Pilate why he came into the world: "For this reason I was born, and for this I came into the world, to testify to the truth. Everyone who is of the truth hears my voice" (Jn 18:37). Pilate appropriately asks, "What is truth?" Notice the question. He did not ask about a particular truth, but rather, he asks about truth *itself*. The question is not about *this* or *that* truth but about universal, eternal Truth. Pilate, as a Roman, would have been trained or at least familiar with the classical teachings of his time, which include the teachings of the ancient Greeks. The Greeks sought to answer, or at least attempted to have a better understanding of, these four universal concepts: the *One*, the *Good*, the *Beautiful*, and the *True*. Unknown to them, these are the four eternal attributes of God. So let me pose Pilate's question once again: "What is truth?" After all, as Christians we want to be *of* the truth to follow Christ: "Everyone who is of the truth hears my voice" (Jn 18:37).

What is the truth? The truth is that Jesus *is* the Truth, and we can only arrive at the truth through him. He himself said at the Last Supper: "I am the way, and the truth, and the life" (Jn 14:6), and it is only through Christ that we find ultimate joy. Jesus is the great *I AM*. He is the very same *I AM* we saw in the Book of Exodus and the one we see in book of Revelation: "I am the Alpha and the Omega" (Rev 22:13). He is the *I AM* that goes beyond space and time, without beginning or end. Jesus Christ is the eternal, universal, and undisputed Truth – the envy of Socrates, Plato, Aristotle, and everyone else that wanted to know Truth, including Pontius Pilate.

As Christians, the only way to the truth is *through* Christ, and the only way to joy and everlasting life is *through* Christ. As Jesus himself tells us: "No one comes to the Father except through me" (Jn 14:6). Jesus *is* Truth. Not a particular truth, or what we think truth is, or what the latest polls or mass majority of people say truth should be. No, Jesus is Truth itself. Only by accepting this truth can we increase in our love for Christ so that we may "discern what is of value, so that [we] may be pure and blameless for the day of Christ, filled with the fruit of righteousness that comes through Jesus Christ" (Phil 1:10). We become righteous by following his way, his commandments, which is the only path to authentically love him. If we follow his way we will arrive at the truth, and with the truth comes joy and eternal life. It is a sobering thought that in his final moments with his apostles, upon his impending capture and death, he prays on their behalf with these words: "Consecrate them in the truth; your word is truth" (Jn 17:17).

Yet, we find out that Pilate was never really interested in the truth. Rather, he was more concerned with finding a pragmatic solution to the situation at hand. Pilate eventually upholds an old Jewish custom of releasing one prisoner during Passover and he allowed the people to choose whom they wanted to be freed. The choice was between Jesus and Barabbas. In his zeal for an independent and free Jerusalem, Barabbas was arrested and imprisoned for killing a Roman soldier. Jesus, however, did not fit this "conquering" messianic description, and therefore wasn't the messiah they wanted: "So the choice is between a Messiah who leads an armed struggle, promises freedom and the kingdom of one's own, and this mysterious Jesus who proclaims that losing oneself is the way to life. Is it any wonder that the crowds prefer Barabbas?"[42] It seems that even today people prefer to impose their own views on who the messiah and what His Church should be, rather than losing themselves and undergoing conversion.

The crowds eventually chose Barabbas over Jesus, and under pressure from the Jewish leaders, Pilate was forced to carry out the sentence of crucifixion. On his way to Calvary (the place of his crucifixion), Jesus fell three times under the weight of the cross. A bystander by the name of Simon of Cyrene was commanded to help Jesus carry his cross. A valuable lesson is given here: although we must all carry our own particular crosses during our earthly pilgrimage, we can never do it alone. We should never undertake the struggles of life on our own. Even in the midst of loneliness and abandonment, we must rely on some type of external help. It is during these trying times that we must ask God to lighten the burden of our own crosses. Reliance on God during these difficult times allows us to receive his overflowing graces, which in turn, helps us to persevere. This is the gift of fortitude.

Upon reaching the hill of crucifixion known as Golgotha (literally meaning *place of the skull*), Jesus was stripped of all his clothing and nailed to the cross. It is during this moment that Jesus becomes most exposed and vulnerable in giving of himself completely for those whom he loves. Amid the temptations and shouts to come down from the cross, he fulfills by his own example the words he had spoken earlier: "No one has greater love than this, to lay down one's life for one's friends" (Jn 15:13). It is from *this* supreme act that the sacrament of the ministerial priesthood flows. His example becomes the model for all those called by him to carry out the mission of his Church. It is here on the cross where God, made man, espoused himself to his Church. It is for this reason that the Mass, which is a remembrance of his Passion and death, is regarded as the "source and summit" of the Church, from which the ministerial priesthood shines forth.[43] Indeed, his mission, his ministry, was accomplished at his death. Whereas the first Adam brought upon death and ruin to humanity through the Tree of the Knowledge of Good and Evil, the New Adam brings about life eternal through the tree of death, now transformed as only he can, to the tree of redemption. It is by his suffering and death that supreme and ultimate love was achieved.

It is therefore a mistake to mirror the sacrificial union of Jesus Christ to his Bride, the Church, with the marriage between a man and a woman. Rather, it is the marriage between a husband and wife that should mirror the Sacrifice of Jesus Christ.[44] This is made possible because through his incarnation and death he became perfectly united with his beloved Bride,[45] after which matrimony is blessed and modeled.[46] Although we all share in the royal priesthood of Jesus Christ by means of our baptism, those who consecrate themselves in the ministerial priesthood by dedicating their lives for the greater service of others as celibates (as is the common practice in the Latin Church), seek directly to imitate the person of Christ in striving for the Kingdom of Heaven by enhancing the sacrificial spirituality of the priesthood. Like all persons who consecrate themselves to God, virginity is "a powerful sign of the supremacy of the bond with Christ and of the ardent expectation of his return, a sign which also recalls that marriage is a reality of this present age which is passing away."[47] This does not mean, however, that marriage is worth any less than the consecrated life or the ministerial priesthood: "Whoever denigrates marriage also diminishes the glory of virginity. Whoever praises it makes virginity more admirable and resplendent."[48] In other words, when you praise and acknowledge the goodness of marriage, you further praise the greatness of virginity. While sacrifices are made under both vocations, Christ makes himself present in the sacrifice of the Mass "in the person of the minister [because] it is the same Christ who formerly offered himself on the cross that now offers [sacrifice] by the ministry of priests ..."[49]

The ministerial priesthood is indeed a special calling. These are the ones sent to gather the harvest. Jesus tells us: "The harvest is plentiful, but the laborers are few; pray therefore the Lord of the harvest to send out laborers into his harvest" (Lk 10:2). In today's day and age, it is essential to pray and encourage men who exhibit these same Christ-like qualities to at least consider the ministerial priesthood. Likewise, those already in formation for the priesthood should also receive encouragement and prayer for they are already being tried by fire like clay in a potter's hands. After all, these men are voluntarily discerning to share in the sufferings of Christ. Their joys will be the joys of Christ; their sorrows will be the sorrows of Christ. They "give themselves to God who is loved above all and, pursuing the perfection of charity in the service of the Kingdom, to signify and proclaim in the Church the glory of the world to come."[50]

By his Crucifixion, Christ establishes the mode of being for all Christians: to be in the service of others. In essence, Christianity is defined by the capacity of its members to love. As he himself said: "This is my commandment, that you love one another as I have loved you" (Jn 15:12). This is how we become authentic Christians. As Benedict XVI tells us, "the true morality of Christianity is love. And love does admittedly run counter to self-seeking – it is an exodus out of oneself, and yet this is precisely the way in which man comes to himself."[51] In every aspect of humanity, no matter what the state may be, whether it is the married life or the consecrated life, we are all called to love in this way. Love is beyond the rational, beyond our imperfections, and beyond the impossible: "Love is the very process of passing over, of transformation, of stepping outside the limitations of fallen humanity … into infinite otherness."[52] When we are concerned more about the needs of others, and therefore step outside the limits of our own individuality for their sake, we break "through into the divine."[53]

This very act of complete self-giving was Christ's consummation on the cross. Here, on the marriage bed of the cross, the bridegroom becomes wedded with his bride, the Church. It can be argued then, that the words, "This is my body, which will be given for you (Lk 22:19)," could very well be considered the wedding vows of Christ to his Bride. Like in matrimony between a husband and wife, the offering of Christ was a total gift of self, although in his particular case, his vows exceed beyond death, for he himself promised: "I am with you always, until the end of the age" (Mt 28:20). Christ's giving of himself to his Bride on the cross, in essence, becomes the model for every Christian marriage: "in this description, the Church, the body of Christ, clearly appears as the second subject of conjugal union, to whom the first subject, Christ, shows the love of one who has loved by giving 'himself to her.' This love is the image and above all the model of the love which a husband must show his wife in marriage, when both are subject to one another 'in the fear of Christ.'"[54] Accordingly, those in the ministerial priesthood must give of themselves in this same way to the Bride of Christ, the Church.

It is his love for his Bride that gives Jesus the strength to surrender himself and undergo the terrible afflictions of his suffering, despite the temptation to come down from the cross. As Jesus weakens and nears his death, he is once again taunted to save himself from the agony. The temptation to come down from the cross works its way in from the crowd, beginning with the bystanders, and makes its way through the chief priests and the scribes until it finally reaches the one sharing in the same punishment as Christ himself, the thief. Here we are given some insight to the inner workings of temptation. We learn that temptation naturally becomes more difficult to overcome as we weaken in the flesh, but as Christ shows us, remaining strong in the spirit ultimately overcomes any and all temptation.

After the thief taunts Jesus to, "Save yourself and us (Lk 23:39)," the other crucified thief immediately rebukes him by saying: "Have you no fear of God, for you are subject to the same condemnation? And indeed, we have been condemned justly, for the sentence we received corresponds to our crimes, but this man has done nothing criminal" (Lk 23:40). The "good thief," as he is now commonly known, shows us something the "bad thief" did not, namely, a repentant heart. He is sorry for the sins he committed, which were probably associated with the uprising of Barabbas. Benedict makes this connection by pointing out that the label "robber" or "thief" was also given to Barabbas in John's gospel, which indicates that these men crucified with Jesus, in all likelihood, were indeed resistance fighters against the Roman Empire and that the term "robber" was imposed to further criminalize them.[55] As the good thief hangs upon the cross, he comes to the realization that he has been following the wrong messiah and that the Kingdom of God cannot be achieved through violence. It is then that he realizes the true messiah in the person of Jesus Christ, which prompts him to say, "Jesus, remember me when you come into your kingdom" (Lk 23:42). Then, acknowledging his change of heart, Jesus turns to the good thief and says in reply, "Amen, I say to you, today you will be with me in Paradise" (Lk 23:43). The good thief, thus, becomes an image of hope, that even in the last hours of our lives we may still receive God's mercy.

Also present at the crucifixion was his very own mother, Mary, the New Eve. As she witnessed his suffering, the prophesy of Simeon was fulfilled,[56] for in her grief, it was as though she was pierced by a sword. As he hung upon the cross, he spoke to her saying, "Woman, behold, your son." Then, looking at his beloved disciple, he said, "Behold, your mother" (Jn 19:26-27). By calling her "woman," Jesus sets her apart as the New Eve, the model for all women, the way the first Eve should have been. Then, handing her over to his beloved disciple, he calls her "mother," for she now becomes the mother of all the members of his Church. If you recall, Jesus had called her "woman" once before at the wedding of Cana. John is clearly making a connection between the wedding at Cana and his crucifixion. The imagery of a wedding is invoked, for just as Eve belonged to Adam in Genesis, so does the New Eve belong to the New Adam at the foot of the Cross. John, by taking her into his care, now becomes her son, and she in turn, becomes his mother. Thus, according to early Church tradition, Mary is seen not only as mother of the New Creation,[i] but the Church as well. The handing over of Mary to the beloved disciple is therefore also seen as Jesus entrusting his Bride, the Church, to those who are in loving communion with himself. This act is to be relived by all of his faithful disciples, as Benedict XVI tells us: "Again and again the disciple is asked to take Mary as an individual and as the Church into his own home and, thus, to carry out Jesus' final instruction."[57] In return, Mary, as mother of the Church, continuously intercedes on our behalf to further unite us with her Son.

Finally, in the ninth hour (three in the afternoon), according to gospel of John, Jesus utters the words, "It is finished" (Jn 19:30) with regards to his mission, and in Luke's gospel he cries out in a loud voice saying, "Father, into your hands I commend my spirit" (Lk 23:46) and he breathed his last breath. Thus occurred the single greatest act in human history; God, made man, died for our salvation, to unite us with his Father in Paradise. So amazed was a centurion who had witnessed the whole thing, that he, a pagan, glorified God and exclaimed, "This man was innocent beyond doubt" (Lk 23:47).

As incredible as the death of Jesus was, it would have been meaningless without the Resurrection. The resurrection of our Lord ushered in a new era in the history of humanity. What was once inaccessible is once again accessible; what was once closed is now open. Paradise has been won for us at a costly price, and now it is our turn to prove ourselves worthy of such an inheritance. This places an obligation on our part to complete the commandments of Christ if we are to be united with Him, the Father, and the saints in heaven. Luckily, he has sent us the Holy Spirit to guide those entrusted with

---

[i] Creation redeemed by Christ's saving act.

administering his teachings and the sacraments[i] in order to help us complete this task. The immediate challenge of our times is how to integrate, and more so, communicate, the Gospel to an increasingly secular culture. Here we must discuss the Christian of today and address the practical ways in which we can truly live out an authentic life in Christ. Only in doing so can we hope to live a life of joy amidst human frailty and suffering.

---

[i] The Magisterium (the teaching office of the Church) and those entrusted with the sacraments (i.e. Holy Orders). Jesus entrusted his teaching authority to his Apostles and their successors, which is seen in Mt 16:19, and Mt 18:18.

Part II

The Christian of Today

Sin & Temptation

There are many challenges and obstacles that are put in our paths as we seek to follow Christ. No one is spared from the temptations that seek to distract us from following God's ways. As we saw in Jesus' own life, not even the Son of God, while he walked among us, was free from temptation. We have seen some of the temptations Christ faced when he hung upon the cross, but here I would like to take a closer look at the first time scripture mentions them, prior to when he began his ministry. I alluded to them earlier, and I promised I would revisit his temptations in the desert because they give us deep insight to the very same temptations we face today. In order for Christ to fully sympathize with humanity it was necessary for him to experience and undergo temptation.

Paul tells us in his letter to the Hebrews that Jesus "had to become like his brothers in every way, that he might be a merciful and faithful high priest before God to expiate the sins of the people. Because he himself was tested through what he suffered, he is able to help those who are being tested" (Heb 2:17-18). As I have said before, Jesus suffered temptations throughout his entire mission, even at the moment of his crucifixion. These temptations "are with him every step of the way."[58] If Jesus was constantly tempted throughout his earthly life, it should be no surprise to us that we would be tempted as well. What is, then, the nature of Jesus' temptations? Jesus, being the most vulnerable person to ever walk the earth, is also subject to the most grueling temptations, which strike at the core of his very identity.

If you recall, immediately following his baptism, Jesus went into the dessert for forty days in preparation for his ministry. During that time, Jesus went through tremendous tests, which sought to attack every aspect of his being. His temptations came in a three step process, each progressively worse than the other. The first temptation strikes at the basic human level: the body. The first temptation being: "If you are the Son of God, command these stones to become loaves of bread" (Mt 4:3). The devil begins with natural bodily cravings. Jesus has been fasting for forty days and is hungry. This temptation, as Benedict points out, is also accompanied by the mockery: "If you are the Son of God..." This small phraseology is loaded with malicious underpinnings. This would not be the last time Jesus would hear these words. Recall the bystanders at the foot of the cross: "if you are the Son of God, come down from the cross!" (Mt 27:40). This phrase strikes at his very identity as Son of God. Essentially, it is a demand for proof. This is a recurring question placed by many who doubt who he is. Even after performing various miracles, many still chose not to believe. They want absolutely no ambiguity or contradiction as Benedict points out.[59] This is a demand that is still placed today by many agnostics and atheists for the existence of God. They will always demand that God show himself to the world, or else they will never believe.[60] It is no wonder then, why many miracles did not occur in towns where Jesus found little faith. Miracles were never intended to be simply signs of power, or solutions to impossible problems, but rather, opportunities for change and conversion. However, the ultimate goal of the temptation is not for us to deny God's existence, but rather to deny ourselves the right to be called sons and daughters of God. The temptation seeks to put doubt to that very claim, and it does so in various ways. For example, many times when people find themselves deep in sin they will tell themselves, "I am not worthy of forgiveness," and they choose not to go and receive the sacrament of Reconciliation. This temptation to avoid the sacrament is essentially the same as denying one's baptismal title of *king*[i] because the underlying thought is, "I am not worthy to be called a son or daughter of God." The temptation seeks to further drive us away from God and his mercy.

After passing the first temptation to break his fast, the second temptation is progressively worse and continues to threaten Jesus'

---

[i] See chapter on Baptism.

mission. The devil takes Jesus to the pinnacle of the temple and tempts him to jump off the ledge by quoting a verse from Psalm 91 in saying: "If you are the Son of God, He will command his angels concerning you; and on their hands they will bear you up, so that you will not strike your foot against a stone" (Mt 4:5). The real essence of this temptation lies in subjecting God to the terms and conditions of the devil's argument. Again, the devil places doubt by trying to have Jesus prove that he is the Son of God. Benedict points out the real issue at stake: "The issue, then, is the one we have already encountered: God has to submit to experiment. He is 'tested,' just as products are tested. He must submit to the conditions that we say are necessary if we are to reach certainty."[61] This is why Jesus responds with the scripture text, "You shall not put the Lord your God to the test" (cf. Dt 6:16). Likewise, must we, too, have to provide some sort of "proof" to be considered sons and daughters of God? If Jesus had accepted the terms imposed on him by the devil, he would cease to be God because he would have given more power to the devil. The devil quotes Psalm 91 completely out of context and devoid of its meaning - of its true message of hope and love. The meaning ultimately lies in trusting God:

> If you follow the will of God, you know that in spite of all the terrible things that happen to you, you will never lose a final refuge. You know that the foundation of the world is love, so that even when no human being can or will help you, you may go on, trusting in the One who loves you. Yet this trust, which we cultivate on the authority of Scripture and at the invitation of the risen Lord, is something quite different from the reckless defiance of God that would make God our servant.[62]

We finally arrive at the third and final temptation in the desert. This temptation strikes at the heart of Jesus' mission, and it will follow him all the way to the cross. The temptation is as follows "the devil took him to a very high mountain, and showed him all the kingdoms of the world and the glory of them; and he said to him, 'All these I will give you, if you will fall down and worship me'" (Mt 7:8-9). The devil shows Christ all the kingdoms of the earth in their splendor. At first glance it would seem this temptation is a temptation of power, but it is much more potent than that. Isn't this what the people of Israel expected from the messiah, to restore the kingdom of Israel and bring all other nations under its dominion? Is this earthly ambition the real focus of this temptation? As we now know, the center of this temptation is, rather, deviation from the cross. The devil will put into our lives all sorts of earthly pleasures as an alternative to our own crosses. It is much easier to fall into these temptations than to follow the path of Christ, which by its very nature involves self-sacrifice. This is the temptation that followed Jesus all the way to the cross, and it will follow us to our own deaths as well. Yet, notice how Jesus never appealed to his divine power to overcome these temptations. He was modeling for us how to defeat temptation by using the authority of scripture in word and action. In short, he overcame temptation with humility – the opposite of pride.

Unfortunately, humility seems hard to come by these days. The truth of the matter is, as human beings, we all fall into sin because we are imperfect beings. We willingly choose pleasure over the greater good, which more than often requires self-sacrifice and self-control. Here I would like to offer practical ways to avoid falling into sin by demonstrating the stages of sin as described by the late Bishop Fulton Sheen. Bishop Sheen was an Emmy award-winning TV personality from the 1960's and 70's. He captured the attention of his audience by preaching the Gospel in a way that was relevant and applicable to all viewers. In one of his episodes, Fulton Sheen provides a useful guide to help us avoid falling into sin and temptation. On a practical level, Fulton Sheen takes a psychological approach towards temptation. He begins with a quote from Oscar Wilde: "I can resist anything but temptation."[63] The quote contains quite a bit of truth. It is, in fact, true that no one can resist temptation, and as we have just seen, neither was Jesus. According to Sheen, there are stages that a person undergoes when temptation enters the mind. There are a series of steps, with regards to sinful acts, that if a person is not careful, could lead to compulsion.

In the mind there are what Sheen likes to call "flammable material."[64] These flammable materials are sex, ego/power, and possessions/property. These impulses that we have are inherently good because they each serve a purpose: Sex for procreation; Ego/power for truth, ambition, spiritual and mental perfection; and possession/property as an external guarantee of our freedom (the freedom to claim something as one's own). These are good in their proper place, but they can be perverted.

Sheen compares these things to fire in a hearth and not on our clothes. Fire in its proper place is a good, but when taken outside its "hearth" it can become destructive. There is nothing wrong with us because we are tempted. This lets us know that we are human. Temptation often comes from the outside, e.g. something we hear, see, desire. As St. Ignatius tells us in his Rules of Discernment, temptations frequently manifest themselves through images in our mind.[65] Rather than feeding these images, we should try to understand where they are coming from.

The first stage according to Sheen is when we consent to the temptation, i.e., when we commit the first act. Under the "flammable material" of sex, we begin to think and rationalize along the lines of, "Everyone is doing it. The morals have changed." We rationalize our immoral behavior because we try to justify and legitimize it. With regards to ego/power we begin to think, "Why should I let someone tell me what to do?" In other words, it becomes a question of obedience. With property, we begin to think we are "entitled," as though we are deserving of our neighbor's goods. Rather than an expression of our external freedom, property can easily draw us into slavery.

The second stage of temptation is habit. Once the act has been committed multiple times it soon becomes a bad habit, or "vice," as the Church calls it. The person continues to commit the same sins over and over to the point where they become accustomed to the action. According to Sheen, "the habit is easy to begin and easy to break." They still have the freedom to quit if the person really desired to do so. They have not yet reached the point of no return.

The third stage is the final stage of temptation. By this point there has been a grave violation of the due order. Sex turns into compulsion. Power turns into tyranny. Property, or possession, turns the person into a kleptomaniac (a person who has an obsessive desire to steal). The agent of the temptation, which before was external to the person, now becomes internal. According to Sheen, the person by this point loses their freedom. The person begins to say, "I'm sick," and indeed they are sick. It is like the alcoholic who has lost the will power to stop drinking. They have succumbed themselves to the disease of alcoholism. This enslavement is a "possession," much like the spiritual possessions that Jesus exercised. The person becomes divided. They want to give up their evil ways but they can't seem to stop. As Sheen points out, they become so divided that, like the demoniac, they come to say, "My name is legion."[66] The person is pulled in different directions. They do things they don't want to do. There is no barrier between the person and the excessive. The person is driven to despair. It is at this point that they feel forgiveness is impossible. They no longer view themselves worthy to be called a son or daughter of God. Many times we ask ourselves, "How could people reach such a wretched level?"[67] This occurs when individuals fall under the guise of apparent freedoms: "This freedom has content, then, it has direction, and it therefore contradicts what only apparently liberates man, but in truth makes him a slave."[68]

Although the person loses their freedom, freedom has not yet been completely destroyed. According to Sheen, You can never drive out a compulsion; you need to "crowd" it out. You must introduce something new. Introduce another love: Divine love. The moment we begin to recognize that there is a Higher Love, from which all other things derive, we can then properly order the goods of our lives. When we recognize the *source* of all our loves and pleasures, as Jesus was able to recognize in his Father, we too can step away from the idols we have created. Fulton Sheen concludes by saying: "We have more temptations to be good than bad," and that is a comforting thought!

As Benedict also reminds us:

> At the heart of all temptations, as we see here, is the act of pushing God aside because we perceive him as secondary, if not actually superfluous and annoying, in comparison with all the apparently far more urgent matters that fill our lives. Constructing a world by our own lights, without reference to God, building on our own foundation; refusing to acknowledge the reality of anything beyond the political and material, while setting God aside as an illusion – that is the temptation that threatens us in many varied forms.[69]

Prayer

The battle against the possessive (i.e. that which takes hold of us and dominates us) requires vigilance, and sobriety of heart.[70] In order to "crowd out" these lesser loves we must introduce a greater love. By our own efforts we cannot hope to achieve sobriety unless we ask God for his graces. In order to have God's divine love intervene, we must first and foremost begin a conversation with that Love, which is precisely what prayer is. As Psalm 27:8 tells us: "'Come,' my heart says, 'seek his face!'" When we focus more on God everything else begins to feel less important, the distractions begin to disperse, and we enter into prayer with a more purified and freer heart. Prayer leads to humility.

Prayer is essential for the Christian person, and as the Catechism explains, "Prayer is both a gift of grace and a determined response on our part. It always presupposes effort."[71] Prayer is a battle. Against whom you might wonder? Against ourselves and against the Tempter who does all he can to turn us away from prayer, away from union with God. The Catechism also says: "We pray as we live, because we live as we pray. If we do not want to act habitually according to the Spirit of Christ, neither can we pray habitually in his name. The 'spiritual battle' of the Christian's new life is inseparable from the battle of prayer."[72] That is why it's essential to set up time to pray and stick to that schedule.

Objections to Prayer

Many people, unfortunately, have a misconception of what prayer is. They think prayer is simply a psychological activity to escape the difficulties of their present lives, or they "reduce prayer to a ritual of words and postures."[73] In reality, prayer is something that goes beyond us, beyond psychology and a simple state of mind. Prayer is a conversation, and there can be no conversation without at least two people. Prayer is a spiritual conversation that helps us reflect upon God and ourselves.

We consciously, and sometimes unconsciously, place barriers to our life of prayer. Often, you hear people say, "We don't have time to pray." Many who seek God in prayer become discouraged because they think prayer is made by their own efforts alone, but in reality prayer comes also from the Holy Spirit. Can you really have a conversation with just yourself and expect an encounter that is radically "other?" It requires both speaking *and* listening. Many times we are eager to tell God what we want, but we sometimes fail to listen and see what *He* wants for us.

If we are not vigilant, we can sometimes fall into the temptation of thinking that unless I have physical proof that prayer is actually meeting my expectations then it cannot be productive. In other words, we sometimes fall into the temptation of thinking that prayer must be profitable, and if it's unproductive, it's useless.[74] Those who think in such a manner regard creature comforts and the pleasures of this world as the criteria for happiness. These are the individuals who pray to win the lottery because they think it will put an end to all their problems and suffering, but how does that benefit their souls? How does that fulfill the void that only God can fill? How does that put an end to their restlessness? True prayer is caught up in the glory of the living and true God, precisely because our hearts were made for God. As St. Augustine once said, "our heart is restless until it rests in you."[75]

As I mentioned before, prayer can seem like a battle. At times it may feel as though nothing is being achieved by praying. What does this look like? We may become discouraged when we experience periods of dryness, when we don't sense anything happening. We may also feel a sense of sadness because we have focused so much on what we don't have or experience that we fail to give ourselves completely to the Lord.[76] We may feel especially disappointed when we feel God is not listening to our own wants and desires. More often than not, we take for granted that prayer is a free and an undeserved gift. We end up asking, "what good does it do to pray?" As the Catechism tells us: "To overcome these obstacles, we must battle to gain humility, trust, and perseverance."[77]

As I pointed out earlier, more often than not, the greatest difficulty in prayer is distraction. Distraction can be a battle in–it–of–itself, and yet, it can be very revealing. Distractions reveal to us what are hearts are attached to. Many times this is the Spirit's way of revealing to us the things that are keeping us from fully loving God. This opens up a great opportunity for us to meditate upon the things we should fast from. Here's a simple example: if a song is "stuck in my head" and is keeping me from concentrating on my prayers, this may be the Spirit's way of telling me to fast from music, at least prior to my time of prayer. Rather than entertaining these distractions, it is best to invite God to enter into our hearts and ask him to purify us from these pleasures so that He may be our one true love. It is not to say that these pleasures are necessarily bad, like in the superficial example I gave, but we must recognize that our greatest pleasure should be found in God who created them, and when it comes to prayer, God should never be compromised with a lesser love. Even St. Augustine struggled with this reality as he himself told God: "And see, you were within and I was in the external world and sought you there, and in my unlovely state I plunged into those lovely things which you made."[78]

Along with distractions, one of the biggest difficulties, especially for those who earnestly want to pray, is dryness. Dryness may feel as though God is absent or distant. It is almost as though there was a void inside of us. This may occur when we fail to internalize the Word of God. When we read scripture are we simply reading words, or are we truly making an effort to understand and internalize what God is trying to tell us? Periods of dryness require more effort: "If dryness is due to the lack of roots, because the word has fallen on rocky soil, the battle requires conversion. The person may be experiencing what's called a 'spiritual desolation.'"[79] Everyone goes through what are called *spiritual consolations* and *desolations*. These are highs and lows that a person experiences in their spiritual life. Some days we may feel very close to God, and other days we may feel as though God is far or even absent, but in both cases, God is indeed very present.

It is very easy for a person to fall into traps when they undergo a spiritual desolation. The mind easily wonders towards things that are "low and earthly,"[80] as St. Ignatius tells us, which is why distractions can be very dangerous. Being in a spiritual desolation is not necessarily a bad thing. It is a sign that the person is moving towards God. During these moments of dryness and loneliness, we should see this as an invitation from God to reach further. Sometimes God steps back so that we can step forward. The effort we put to reach further will not only help us grow closer to God, but in the process, make us holier men and women. During moments of spiritual desolation, it is best to never make a change to your spiritual life.[81] Remain faithful to your life of prayer. If anything, add to it. Ask God for the grace of perseverance. When the desolation is over think about all the graces you have received during your struggle and remember what you have learned for the next time it occurs.

From Love to Lust

Unfortunately, too often people prefer to rationalize their immoral behavior to justify their way of living instead of undergoing inward discernment. The good Spirit continues to gnaw at their consciences but they willingly choose to ignore it. They would rather not leave their life of comfort, no matter how damaging this may be to their inner peace. Even when confronted by others, neither reason, nor common sense will change their minds for the simple matter that they do not like to be told what to do: "People are accustomed to a particular sort of life, and when this is threatened, they of course put up resistance."[82]

This may explain why some people choose not to follow certain teachings of the Church. More often, they have false notions of the Church's teachings, thinking the Church to be controlling and placing restrictions on their "freedoms," when in reality, the Church seeks to free them from the slavery of sin and guilt. As Bishop Fulton Sheen points out: "The priest must try to discover if the objections against the faith expressed by an inquirer are in fact intellectual or if instead they are basically moral, that is, rooted in some improper behavior. It is important to find out not only what people say about the Christ and His Church, but why they say it."[83]

Perhaps we may know someone within our own family, or a close friend, who falls under this category. Many times we want to instruct them and teach them how living out the teachings of the Church leads to happiness, and yet, at the same time, we must be careful not to argue with them for fear of further driving them away from the faith as Sheen also points out: "Instructing is not arguing. One can win an argument and lose a soul ... If we believed the lies they believe about the Church, we would hate her a thousand times more than they."[84] Sometimes the best thing we can do is entrust these individuals to God through our prayers. Only God has the power to truly move hearts, and as we pray for those we love, we must also pray for ourselves to grow in patience, much like St. Monica, who prayed unceasingly for many, many years for the conversion of her son, St. Augustine.

Either way, the issue at hand is the primacy of God. Is God truly at the center of our lives, or do we place these "apparent" freedoms first and foremost? Pope Benedict addressed this when he stated: "The issue is acknowledging he [God] is a reality, that he is the reality without which nothing else can be good."[85] Too often, God is ignored, or at best, a secondary thought in people's lives. Scripture, in turn, simply becomes a work of literary history and irrelevant to contemporary life. The Bible is treated this way because by its very nature scripture demands conversion and self-sacrifice, which many refuse to undergo. As a result, people mutilate scripture to have it conform to their own lifestyle: "And so the Bible no longer speaks of God, the living God; no, now *we* alone speak and decide what God can do and what we will and should do."[86] The same occurs with regards to Church teaching. People will accept and reject as they please while still maintaining their so-called "Catholic" identity. In reality, not only are they abandoning their core beliefs, but in practicality, they are creating their own little schismatic churches. Pope Francis has spoken strongly towards these Christians:

> This is why we "have to be careful not to slide toward that path of pagan Christians, Christians in appearance". In reality, "the temptation to adapt to mediocrity—the mediocrity of these Christians—is actually their downfall, because the heart cools, it becomes lukewarm". But "the Lord speaks a strong word to the lukewarm: 'because you are lukewarm, I will spew you out of my mouth'". These people, the Pontiff repeated, "are enemies of the Cross of Christ: they take the name, but don't follow the requirements of Christian life".[87]

It seems the sins most rationalized today seem to be those with regard to human sexuality, partly because the subject itself is heavily misunderstood. People try to justify the improper use of their sexuality by presenting their behavior as "normal," "liberating," and even going as far as calling it "love." When in reality, their sexual practices are "unnatural," "enslaving," and "lustful." It seems this is the most frequent topic of discussion today, which in a way is unsurprising considering the Sexual Revolution has now reached its full maturation. The Sexual Revolution of the 1960's and the nation-wide acceptance of the contraceptive pill has formally divorced sexual intercourse from marriage, the implications of which are astronomical. Rather than a man and a women giving of themselves fully and without reservations, as in marriage, they now carelessly use each other for sexual favors without the responsibility of having to raise children, or even undertaking the role of caring and providing for one another, as occurs in what is dubbed "casual sex."

Why is contraception considered such an evil when the majority of people are using them? Why are these people indifferent to the Church's teachings, as Pope Frances pointed out? Why are they so ardent on making sure they do not conceive children? Is it a question of finance? And what happens when contraception fails? Is abortion the only solution? Bishop Robert W. Finn of Kansas City tells us exactly what is at the root of the problem:

> Why is this so terribly amiss? Because the foundation and cause of abortion is not poverty but a blind disregard for personal responsibility, a heinous denial and disrespect for human life, and an idolatrous worship of personal convenience. This is why even in the wealthy countries of Scandinavia the highest rates of abortions are followed by rampant euthanasia.[88]

The issue at hand is the disregard of human dignity in favor of self-idolization. In other words, we make ourselves the center of our own universes with little to no regard for the needs and wellbeing of others, causing us to cringe and lash-out when infringements get in the way of our desires – transforming and perverting us into self-worshipping idols. With this much self-adoration we negate authentic love from others and fail to worship the one true God. Love without sacrifice and responsibility is lust, and it only shows the immaturity present within the individual.

The effects of the Sexual Revolution have seriously distorted the meaning of love. The false notion that contraceptives, such as the pill, give us more liberty is in fact the complete opposite of what liberty really is. Instead, it places conditions on love itself. These conditions manifest themselves in the following ways: "I will only love you if … we don't have children; we don't have commitments; the pleasure lasts, etc." This is a false liberty rooted in the slavery of one's passions, rather than the liberty one finds in the total gift of self without limits or conditions. Too often, the notion of love is equated with, "how much can I get?" instead of, "how much can I give?" One only has to do a survey on how many people use contraceptives and/or cohabitate outside of marriage to confirm this reality. Even within marriage, the use of artificial contraception falsely introduces the concept of sexual intercourse without responsibility. This notion, simply put, is nothing more than casual sex within marriage. The conjugal act itself is a sacred act, but removed from its true purpose and meaning, becomes sacrilegious. It is no wonder, then, why the number of divorces has drastically increased since 1973.

Interestingly enough, the pill was actually approved by the FDA as a means to control menstrual disorders in woman and not as a contraceptive. It was not long after its approval that the pill was adopted as the widespread means of birth control just as the "free love" (a.k.a. casual sex) movement was in full swing (no pun intended). The pill was supposed to be the so-called solution to reduce the abortion rate. Yet, not only did the pill not reduce abortions, it encouraged more frequent casual sex, and since its legalization in 1973, the number of abortions to date is almost at 60 million in the United States alone.[89] Proponents of abortion argue its legality under the claim that the beginnings of a human person is unknowable, or immeasurable to a certain degree, and therefore should be upheld in favor of the mother's convenience. This argument holds no ground since neither can they disprove the point at which a human person comes into being. All that can be agreed upon is that prior to conception there can be no person. Since after conception it cannot be disproved that there is not a unique human person within the mother, that fetus (lit. "young one" in Latin) should have the rights, privileges and protection of the law. Therefore, to execute the life within the womb based simply on the suspicion that it may not be a unique human person, without scientific proof, should be considered illegal.

Being in favor of the dignity of the human person in the midst of this scientific obscurity, the Church holds a person comes into being at the moment of conception. For proponents of abortion, convenience trumps understanding. In the end, however, life cannot be legislated. Why let politicians tell us what is morally right? Why stand in the sidelines and let them dictate and legislate what is truth? As I mentioned before, truth is not something conceived by an individual or group of individuals, but something beyond us, something which does not contradict reason, something found in logic, in the *Logos*, in the eternal Word we call God. Morality, thus, is a personal duty, not an idea that we accept or reject based on personal convenience. It is, in short, a responsibility to do what is good in conformity with reason. The minute we make ourselves masters over what is right and wrong based upon our own human judgment, is the minute we put our own human dignity in peril.

The Catholic Church has always held the sanctity of life at every stage decades before the Sexual Revolution even took place, as evident in Pope Pius XI's 1930 *Casti Connubii*:

> Since, therefore, openly departing from the uninterrupted Christian tradition some recently have judged it possible solemnly to declare another doctrine regarding this question, the Catholic Church, to whom God has entrusted the defense of the integrity and purity of morals, standing erect in the midst of

the moral ruin which surrounds her, in order that she may preserve the chastity of the nuptial union from being defiled by this foul stain, raises her voice in token of her divine ambassadorship and through Our mouth proclaims anew: any use whatsoever of matrimony exercised in such a way that the act is deliberately frustrated in its natural power to generate life is an offense against the law of God and of nature, and those who indulge in such are branded with the guilt of a grave sin (no. 56).

Today, it seems the topic of contraception has been closed to any real discussion due to its widespread acceptance and prevalent use in our hyper-sexualized culture. In other words, we have become numb to the dangers of contraception because society has deemed it as "normal" and even "necessary." likewise, this same society views something as natural as conception as a "mistake" and a "problem" because it places demands on the individual's liberty. We continue to punish our own bodies for doing what they are naturally supposed to do.

Not only are we punishing our bodies by using artificial contraception, but because sex is now severed from procreation, pleasure therefore becomes the basis for any relationship – both in and outside of marriage. This is why cohabitation or "trial marriages" fail. Without the foresight to see the commitment involved in rearing and raising children, as well as the commitment involved in supporting and tending a spouse, which goes beyond pleasure, the relationship cannot hope to survive. One *New York Times* article states:

> Couples who cohabit before marriage (and especially before an engagement or an otherwise clear commitment) tend to be less satisfied with their marriages—and more likely to divorce—than couples who do not. These negative outcomes are called the cohabitation effect.[90]

However, no matter how many facts or statistics are presented, many people seem to choose immediate pleasure over truth. For those who cohabitate, there is no significant difference between having sex before marriage and on their wedding night. This approach not only perverts the relationship prior to the marriage, but also demolishes any notion of chastity once in it.

Chastity is often mistaken for celibacy (i.e. abstinence from marriage and sexual relations), when in reality chastity is defined as follows:

> Chastity means the successful integration of sexuality within the person and thus the inner unity of man in his bodily and spiritual being. Sexuality, in which man's belonging to the bodily and biological world is expressed, becomes personal and truly human when it is integrated into the relationship of one person to another, in the complete and lifelong mutual gift of a man and a woman.[91]

In other words, chastity is sexuality expressed *both* in body and in spirit as a gift within a lifelong commitment (e.g. marriage). That is why this unity is opposed to any behavior or thing, like artificial contraception, that would impair it.[92] Since sexuality is a gift freely given among spouses, it is clear, then, that there cannot be any room for selfish people within marriage.

What about married couples who aren't ready to have children? First of all, it must be mentioned that marriage is naturally directed towards procreation. Therefore, a couple must seriously keep this in mind prior to entering into matrimony. That being said, there must be a serious reason for a married couple to withhold from having children. Having fewer children to maintain a life of luxury does not count as a "serious" reason. However, the Church, in conformity with natural law, understands that there are responsible occasions for delaying or momentarily abstaining from having children. It is for this reason that the Church encourages the practice of Natural

Family Planning (NFP).[i] NFP (or the Billings Method) is a natural God given way of avoiding pregnancy by looking at the menstrual cycle of a woman to determine periods of fertility and infertility. This method is in accordance with God's will because there is nothing artificial or unnatural interfering with the transmission of life. When practiced correctly, NFP is not only safe, but extremely accurate as well. Bishop Galeone, retired bishop of the diocese of St. Augustine, had this to say:

> Studies have shown that NFP, when accurately followed, can be 99% effective in postponing pregnancy. That's equivalent to the pill and better than all the barrier methods. Best of all, while complying with God's will, husband and wife discover the beautifully designed functions of their fertility, enhance their intimacy, and deepen their love for each other.[93]

During periods of fertility within the menstrual cycle, couples practicing NFP who want to avoid a pregnancy are strongly encouraged to remain abstinent from sexual intercourse as an opportunity to re-enkindle their chaste love for one another. By doing so, the art and tradition of courting continues well into the marriage. It gives the husband an opportunity to once again woo his bride. This practice keeps the marriage fresh by allowing couples to step beyond the routine and create new ways to romance one another. This approach grants pleasure in all three levels of the human person: body, mind, and spirit. The Christian must address his physical, psychological and spiritual needs to be fully whole and healthy. When one of these three is out of balance, so too, does the human person become imbalanced. When those who use artificial contraception are faced with "the routine," they resort to behaviors that strictly remain on the physical level. These behaviors manifest

---

[i] For more information on Natural Family Planning please visit their website: http://nfpandmore.org

themselves in a wide array of perverse acts, such as "role play," which involves dressing up and acting out sexual fantasies because pleasure is no longer found in the *person* of their spouse but in the intensity of their sexual appetite. They prefer to pretend to be with someone else than with each other. They must constantly come up with new ways to outdo the previous behavior. When the desired pleasure is not achieved, the relationship begins to strain and dissolve. This occurs because the relationship is fundamentally rooted in lust, not love. When the person becomes bored with their partner they begin to look for another. This vicious cycle destroys families, and with it, the fabric of society. This helps explain why few marriages make it to "... till death do us part."

What about those with guilt or shame who want to return to a life of purity? Many of these people feel as though there is no going back. They consider themselves ugly, dirty, incapable of being loved. This is a lie from the Evil One. The truth is that purity is reclaimable and achievable. THERE IS HOPE! There is what is called "spiritual virginity." Virginity is never limited to a physical reality. There is always room for conversion. There is always time to start anew. Spiritual virginity involves conversion of the heart, to start a new life in Christ. I personally know many couples that were not chaste prior to entering into marriage, yet their love for God and for each other drove them to give up their promiscuous lifestyles until they were willing to completely give of each other in their totalities (mind, body, & soul). By purifying their hearts, these couples grew in their capacity to love and receive love. Many times these couples become great counselors and evangelizers for other couples struggling with similar temptations. More than ever, the world desperately needs more couples like these that can bear witness to true Christian love. It *is* possible for a woman to regain her purity; it *is* possible for a man to regain his authentic manhood!

Unfortunately, what we continue to find are those who support intrinsic evils while claiming to maintain a so-called Christian identity. People who speak of God and consider themselves Christians, yet commit actions contrary to core Christian beliefs, such as contraception, cohabitation and so on, are not only abandoning their own faith in practice, but by doing so have "obscured the image of God and has opened the doors to disbelief."[94] For the non-believer, there is no reason to believe in the faith of those who constantly negate what they profess if the example they give is no different from what secular society already offers. Rather than drawing people closer to God, these "Christians" drive them further away:

> The man who claims, "I have known him," without keeping his commandments, is a liar; in such a one there is no truth. But whoever keeps his word, truly has the love of God been made perfect in him. The way we can be sure we are in union with him is for the man who claims to abide in him to conduct himself just as he did (1 Jn 2:3-6).

At the heart of the problem is the issue of faith. Do we really believe? Imagine if Jesus had posed contemporary society with the same question he once asked his disciples: "Who do the crowds say that I am (Lk 9:18)?" Or better yet, "who do you say that I am (Lk 9:20)?" Can we honestly look at today's society and respond the same way Peter did? Can we, as a Christian people, respond by saying that Jesus is truly and undeniably "the Messiah of God (Lk 9:20)?" Because in all practicality, a large majority of people act as though Christ didn't even exist. It boggles the mind to hear people say they believe in Jesus and yet ignore his teachings. What do they believe in then? Again, the question is posed: "Who do the crowds say that I am?" Is Jesus an idea, a philosophy, or perhaps an inspirational figure taken from the pages of history? In reality, Jesus should be our life, our hope, and our everything – the very definition of what it means to be a Christian, a follower of the Risen Lord.

This lack of faith has caused the world to deny or ignore anything that cannot be physically seen. The reason why abortion is so rampant is because we are not confronted face to face with the unborn. Faith is belief and trusting in something without having to see it.

Pope Benedict brings up a good point: "Why is infanticide almost unanimously rejected today, whereas we have become virtually inured to abortion? Perhaps the only reason is that in the case of abortion, one does not see the face of the one condemned never to see the light of day."[95] Some people seem to doubt the genuineness of life because they do not *see* it. Here we can apply what Jesus told Thomas when he had previously doubted the Resurrection: "Blessed are those who have not seen and have believed" (Jn 20:29). To some extent, both the unborn and the resurrection of Christ require a leap of faith because in both cases we are not directly confronted with the face of the other.

Before we can love someone, there must be an encounter. To know is to love. This is true whether it be between man and God or among humanity. This is perhaps why the unborn, the marginalized and the poor continue to be largely ignored. It would be an injustice, on our part, if we were to encounter and experience their suffering and still remain indifferent:

> My obligation to be responsive to my neighbor not only forbids me to hurt him positively, it also forbids me from being indifferent to him, to comport myself in my neighbor's presence as if here were not there, to pass him by as if he were some mere thing. When you, my neighbor, here before me, are in distress, I cannot be unconcerned or refuse you reasonable help without equivalently negating your existence as a person. By omitting the response I owe you, I wrong you. I withhold something which, by reason of my nature as a person, you have a right to expect from me, something which is your due. I therefore fail, not merely in charity, but in justice, which requires that I treat you in the same way I wish to be treated myself.[96]

The problem that occurs most often, with regards to helping our neighbor, however, is the lack of spiritual consideration when offering aid. The mentality to address the physical needs of the human person, while disregarding the spiritual, falls very much in line with those who support artificial contraception. When these individuals want to offer aid to the poor they tend to disregard God and everything pertaining to the spiritual dimension of humanity for seemingly more important matters. Temporal matters, therefore, take precedence over spiritual ones:

> When God is regarded as a secondary matter that can be set aside temporarily or permanently on account of more important things, it is precisely these supposedly more important things that come to nothing. It is not just the negative outcome of the Marxist experiment that proves this.[97]

Many Christians turn to Mathew 5:3, which says "Blessed are the poor..." to justify the preeminence of temporal aid, when in reality the full text of Matthew's Gospel says, "Blessed are the poor in spirit." The preeminence is clearly that of a spiritual matter, not simply a material one. This is not to say that material aid is of no importance. However, when material aid takes priority, we endanger ourselves, as Pope Benedict stated, of becoming a Marxist society. This is a danger many nations spread to underdeveloped countries: "The aid offered by the West to developing countries has been purely technical and materially based, and not only has left God out of the picture, but has driven men away from God."[98] Considering the number of dangers I have already mentioned regarding contraception and abortion, developed countries, such as the United States, continue to promote and insist on the use of these dangers in places like Africa, where AIDS continues to spread no matter how many condoms and birth control pills are provided. As stated previously, these methods do nothing more than promote promiscuity. Instead of spending millions of dollars on these intrinsic evils, these nations should promote more effective methods such as abstinence, systematic NFP, and ecological breastfeeding. The reason they will not promote these natural methods is because they are under the impression that every human being has the right to have sex with whomever they want, whenever they want it, and as often as they want it. This not only spreads sexually transmitted diseases and destroys families, but even worse, it destroys morality and the human spirit.

Rather than promoting true progress for the human race, these deceitful ideologues are treating individuals as mere animals. Since they are only concerned with addressing temporal issues through the use of material means, their "services" are likewise no different than routinely feeding and neutering dogs and cats. Their lack of concern for family unity, religious tolerance, and human dignity further highlights this point. For them, sexuality defines the human person. Everything is addressed in genital terms. This is precisely why they are so adamant about promoting the homosexual lifestyle, contraceptive use, and abortion. They completely ignore the other two aspects of the human person, i.e. the psyche and the spiritual. These aspects are what ultimately separate us from the animals. Without a complete understanding of the human person morality ceases to exist.

The truth is, we are all poor. We are all lacking in one way or another. Poverty has many different faces: loneliness, depression, desolation, addiction, despair, etc. No matter how wealthy a person may be, they will always feel a sense of emptiness. This emptiness can only be filled by God's love. The poor are "blessed" because they have much to teach us. They teach us that we are dependent on God and nothing more. The only cure for the poverty in each of us is the love that God can give. This is true of those married, single, religious, rich, poor, and everyone in between. The way we approach our husbands, our wives, our human family, must always be in relation to God himself. Under the eyes of God, despite the many facets of life, we are all equal.[99]

Atheism & Agnosticism

In this last chapter, I would like to discuss the three greatest threats to Christianity. These three groups are a culmination of all the greatest problems facing our Judeo-Christian society. Though the title of this chapter is *Atheism & Agnosticism*, the third threat is almost as damaging. I am, of course, speaking of fundamentalism. All three are an imbalanced view of the world because they are rooted in misguided philosophies.

In this chapter I hope to break down these three positions and point out the errors from which they stem. Why did I decide to include this particular topic as the last chapter of this book? The answer is quite simple: every Catholic by virtue of his or her baptism was given the divine command to, "Go into the whole world and proclaim the gospel to every creature" (Mk 16:15). In the process of carrying out this mission, the faithful Catholic will undeniably encounter resistance from one, if not all, of these groups. If they are to face these challenges, it is important for them to be prepared and rooted in the truth of their faith. As I mentioned before, the greatest problem among Catholics is lack of proper education. It is for this reason that the Catholic individual must at least be familiar with the arguments and errors of these three groups.

First of all, what is the fundamental problem with these three groups? The problem lies in the amount of truth they accept or reject. None of the three accept the truth in its entirety. The truth consists of both faith and reason. Using reason, we can come to know some of the truth by studying the observable universe. We call this study *science*. Through science we can come to arrive at what is called *natural law*. Natural law uses reason to let us know the difference between right and wrong within the natural order of things. For example, in order for a species of animal to procreate, unless that species is asexual, natural law dictates that there must be one female and one male of that particular species to reproduce. By strictly using natural law, we can see that homosexuality is not a natural but rather unnatural inclination because it does not achieve the goal of reproduction. Theology further articulates why this action is immoral by using reason to show how this act does not coincide with God's divine plan. Ultimately, morality is always directed towards the will of God because he is the creator of all that is natural and supernatural.

However, science falls short of knowing the fullness of truth because it is limited by what it can observe. Science must depend on the scientific method (i.e. form a hypothesis, test hypothesis, and form a conclusion) in order to determine a particular truth. Not all truths can be measured using the scientific method. When there is a lack of facts or evidence, science poses a theory (an educated guess) in attempts to explain an unanswered problem. Science, therefore, only deals with what can be perceived by human senses. Science, without guidance, can be misused. In humanity's quest for efficiency, technology (applied science) can favor pragmatism over human dignity. This leads to the justification of using any means necessary to appease the majority, or so-called "common good." This introduces the erroneous idea of using evil to achieve a good. This is a false concept because nothing inherently good can ever be achieved using evil means. This philosophy undermines the dignity of the individuals within a minority. For example: it is much more efficient to destroy an entire village infected with a new airborne virus by bombing it (technology), than spending countless weeks or months of research and resources to find a cure. Science is not only limited in knowing truth, but as I have just demonstrated, without guidance it can be morally insufficient as well.

The problem with atheism, specifically scientific atheism, is that because it chooses to disregard the existence of God, man himself becomes the arbiter of morality. If humanity is nothing more than a by-product of cosmic chaos (as some of them argue), then justice itself is also nothing more than a by-product of the dominant. More than likely, the everyday Catholic will encounter an ignorant atheist, as opposed to an educated scientific atheist. The ignorant atheist will borrow arguments from scientific atheists not because they are in search of truth, but because they oppose the infringements placed by religion. Strictly speaking, these individuals are known as agnostics. Agnostics do not necessarily reject the notion of God, however, they prefer to remain in a state of ignorance rather than pursue the truth. Simply put, they don't know and they don't care to know (literally: *a* (not) + *gnostic* (know)). They prefer to live out their lives without having to face the reality of the truth and the demands it imposes on humanity. By so doing, they are in many ways worse than atheists because they reject and accept truths based on personal convenience.[i]

We are the only physical beings in the known universe to have rationality. From the moment we are born we seek to understand. In those first formative years of our childhoods we approach the world with awe and wonder. Somewhere along the way we begin to lose that childlike approach to our surroundings. Things cease to amaze us, and what was once a mystery, now simply becomes a problem to solve. Scientific Atheists are individuals who want to solve all of life's mysteries using empirical methods, i.e. the scientific method. The problem with this, however, is that some mysteries cannot be solved with a scientific approach. In fact, the true nature of a mystery contradicts the notion that it is something to be solved. This is what makes it different from a problem. A problem seeks to be solved, whereas a mystery seeks to be contemplated. I make this distinction because too often scientific atheists reach beyond their respective fields and meddle with mysteries that should be left in the realm of philosophy. For example, it is not the place of a scientist to determine the reality of justice, love, morality, or the existence of God. These entities cannot be determined using empirical data because they exist beyond physical realities. For the believer, suspicion should be raised when a self-proclaimed atheist injects himself/herself in a discussion that is beyond their field of study.

---

[i] cf. Aquinas, *Summa Theologiea*, I-II, q. 77, a. 4.
Self-love, in the end, is the root of all sin.

The first argument against the existence of God made by atheists that I wish to discuss is what is known as the *Cosmological Argument*. This argument has to do with the creation of the known universe. Unfortunately, many fundamentalist groups misrepresent Christianity because they reject the truths that atheists accept, namely, those given to us by reason (science). Fundamentalists take every word in the Bible and interpret them literally. This is a major problem because not every word in the Bible is meant to be taken and understood as it appears. As I mentioned in the first chapter of this book, certain truths are best conveyed through *mythos*, i.e. storytelling. Storytelling appeals to every generation, and in their simplicity, become timeless conveyers of truth. Many of these extravagant stories like the Creation in Genesis, or the apocalyptic writings of *Revelation*, are more concerned with conveying these truths to the masses rather than a small group of intellectuals. The larger–than–life occurrences in these stories help transmit and reinforce the message of the truth. This is where the use of human reason comes in. It is a great danger for a person to blindly interpret scripture without at least being familiar with the history, context, literary devices, and traditions from which they stem. By removing the lenses of human rationale, fundamentalist groups greatly reduce the messages and meanings contained in scripture. Worse still, by disregarding tradition they leave interpretation to the individual reader, which paves the way for hundreds and thousands of different misinterpretations. In doing so, the truth becomes whatever the individual feels it is, making the real truth obscure and inaccessible. This is the reason why there are hundreds of different Christian religions today.

Atheists love to pounce on these fundamentalists and use their own contradictions as proof for the non–existence of God. Luckily, for us Catholics, we still hold strongly to the traditions passed down to us since the dawn of Christianity, which embrace both faith and reason. As Pope John Paul II said:

> Faith and reason are like two wings on which the
> human spirit rises to the contemplation of truth; and
> God has placed in the human heart a desire to know
> the truth—in a word, to know himself—so that, by
> knowing and loving God, men and women may also
> come to the fullness of truth about themselves.[100]

This is important to understand because many atheists address the literal interpretation of scripture, with regards to the creation of the universe, as a point of contention. They point out, using science, how it is physically impossible for the universe to have been created in 6 days, as the fundamentalists believe. Yet, we must keep in mind that for an atheist to be a true scientist, he must adhere to the laws of physics. The moment he begins to move away from scientific fact and enters into a philosophical argument his credibility as a scientist quickly begins to wane. It's like having a lawyer perform surgery and a surgeon practice jurisprudence. With this in mind, let us look at the cosmological argument for the existence of God.

The Church has always had many bright thinkers and teachers throughout her long history. One of these bright individuals was Fr. Georges Lemaitre, a Belgian physicist, who proposed the Big Bang Theory.[101] Yes, it was a Catholic priest who came up with the Big Bang Theory! The Big Bang Theory implies that our universe had a beginning where there was no physical reality prior to it.[102] This also means that there was no time prior to the Big Bang. Most scientists believe the Big Bang was the initial starter of a large chain of reactions that led to the existence of our known universe. Very few people would dispute that. According to the Big Bang model, the universe began with a huge explosion that set everything in motion for the creation of our universe and the various bodies contained within it. These bodies include the stars, solar systems, planets, asteroids, space dust and everything else within the universe. These bodies are shaped by certain laws in physics such as the law of gravity and quantum mechanics (the physics behind subatomic particles such as the electron).

We are not disputing these scientific laws because these laws are based on fact. In other words, they have been proven using the scientific method of affirming or falsifying a theory. When a theory is proven to be true, it naturally becomes a law. This discussion is not about the observable universe, but rather, what cannot be seen or explained. Therefore, I will not be addressing the specific laws of the universe because it does not directly pertain to the argument at hand, namely, the existence of God. The clash between atheists and theists is ultimately about providing an explanation for the mysteries of the universe beyond the limits of science. The primary question atheists and theists seek to answer is, "why are we here?" Both groups have very different approaches.

The only common denominator between these two groups is that both accept what has already been proven by science (fundamentalists excluded). Both, for the most part, accept the Big Bang model as the origin of the universe. The question then becomes, "what happened before the Big Bang? Was it necessary for an intelligent being (i.e. God) to create the universe and everything in it?" This is essentially what both groups are trying to prove or disprove. Both sides require a leap of faith. Atheists have several theories at their disposal, although most are based on unfounded evidence, some scientific, others, shall we say, imaginative. Theists, on the other hand, take into account the sheer improbability of a system capable of sustaining life. The counter argument to this theistic approach made by atheists involves an "unlimited possibility" scenario, where given an infinite number of possibilities there could exist life outside our own universe. This is where ideas such as multiverse, string theory and parallel universes arise, but are these theories closer to fact or fiction?

First of all, I would like to remind the reader that we are dealing with what is beyond our known universe, beyond what we can see and test. One of the most popular theories discussed today deals with the notion that everything is pre-determined by a series of physical laws. According to this theory, following the Big Bang, a set of physical laws were set which would create the blue prints for any and all activity in the universe. As Hawking wrote: "It is a deterministic universe:

Once you set up a starting configuration, or initial condition, the laws determine what happens in the future."[103] I mention this theory because it undermines free will. In fact, according to this theory, there is no free will. Our so-called "free will" is nothing more than the arrangement of atoms and the laws that govern them, which produces my physical reality. Our actions are impulses determined by our chemical and psychological makeup. We are simply reacting to these chemical reactions, making free will an illusion.

If this is the case, I as "I" would cease to exist. If the cosmos is limitless in possibilities, and there are indeed parallel universes or multiverses, then in theory, through the laws that govern them, I could have an alter ego or an alternate existence in another universe. I, as an individual, cease to exist because there would be various versions of myself spread throughout the cosmos. Justice, likewise, would also cease to exist. If I commit a crime in another universe would I be responsible for those crimes in this universe? In fact, would they be considered crimes at all if my actions were predetermined by the impulses of my chemical makeup? Love itself would also cease to exist because I do not choose whom to love, but rather, I am reacting to my impulses. If this sounds absurd, it's because it is! This particular theory is more a challenge to my common sense than my belief in the Resurrection.

We are not products of random events. We are not orphans. Let me repeat myself: there is no empirical hard evidence to support the above theory. In fact, the conditions that must be met for a universe to not only sustain life, but to create life, are so small that one can't help but conclude that there must have been an Intelligent Design, a Creator:

> The odds of our anthropic universe arising amidst the total phase-space volume of possible universes for a creation event is so exceedingly, exceedingly, exceedingly remote that its notation in regular exponential form is one part in: $10^{10000000000000000000000}$
> 00000000000000000000000000000000000000000000000000000000000000000000000000

00000000000000000000000000000000000000. This number is so large that if we were to write it out in ordinary notation (with every zero being, say, ten point type), it would fill up a large portion of the universe![104]

That's a lot of zeros! According to that figure, we shouldn't even be alive right now. This is why many physicists have come to the conclusion that there must be an Intelligent Design. There is more to suggest the hand of God in our universe than trusting in Stephen Hawking's M-theory. It almost seems as though many atheists, out of desperation to disprove God's existence, will come up with the most farfetched arguments. It takes a greater leap of faith for me to believe in these theories than to place my faith in the existence of God.

Moving from cosmological arguments to philosophical arguments, perhaps the strongest philosophical argument for the non-existence of God made by atheists lies in the question, "why do good people suffer?" This is a question that has resonated for thousands of years. A prime example of this is found in the book of Job in the Old Testament wisdom literature. In it, Job, a just and righteous man, lost everything: his property, his stock, his servants, and even his children. Moreover, he also suffered from bodily illnesses. Job struggles as he questions and doubts his own faith. This is similar to our own day and age when the world wondered where God was during some of the most horrific catastrophes of the past few decades, such as the Holocaust, the hurricane that hit Haiti, the tsunami that hit Japan, or the typhoon that struck the Philippines. Did all these people die senselessly?

As Job struggled to find an explanation for his sufferings, three of his friends approached him and attempted to provide answers. Unfortunately, they approached the matter with a "retribution or recompense theology."[105] In other words, they believed all these bad things were happening to him because he must have done something wrong. Even though Job never did anything wrong, they wanted him to admit to committing offenses against God so that his wealth and prosperity could be restored. If Job were to admit to an offense he never committed, it would prove that his faith was based not on his love for God, but on his love for possessions. This erroneous notion of pleasing God to avoid suffering is called a *theology of prosperity*. This is the very same approach that Satan used to accuse Job before God. He wanted to demonstrate that Job's faithfulness was based on his prosperity, and not on his love for the Lord. I remember seeing on the news a number of Protestant leaders use this reasoning to explain the disaster caused by Hurricane Katrina. They blamed the sinfulness of the Louisiana population for invoking "God's wrath." On the opposite end of the spectrum, atheists used this opportunity to show that this event proves that a benevolent God does not exist. Both groups, whether knowingly or unknowingly, made the same accusatory arguments that Satan and Job's friends had used.

These events may make us feel as though God is unconcerned with the sufferings of humanity, as Job himself felt, but this is far from the truth. Before we dive deeper into the mystery of human suffering, we must explore the meaning and significance of fidelity. Other than questioning the meaning of suffering, faithfulness seems to be the main topic of discussion within the book of Job. I feel it is important for us to ask ourselves this very same question: "What motivates us to remain faithful?" In the story, "Satan basically asked the question, is it love or is it self-serving greed that motivates a person to be righteous, to fear God, and to be separate from sin?"[106] The danger of doing good with the expectation of being rewarded leads to a pragmatic view of religion.[107] In other words, religion is only important as far as I can see and gain results. In question is our love for God *as* God.

Satan's main objective is to have humanity turn its back on God when difficult situations arise. How often do we blame God when bad things happen to us? In the story, Satan had convinced God to allow these terrible things to happen in order to prove that Job's faithfulness was absent of real authentic love. Here we see a glimpse of Satan's true malice against God and humanity. As Larry Waters points out: "It is interesting that God's charge against Satan, 'You incited me against him to ruin him without any reason' (2:3b, NIV), is a horrifying, yet enlightening look into the character of Satan. Humanity means no more to the Accuser than a vehicle for cursing God."[108]

Returning to the subject of human suffering, a sense of hopelessness, despair, and even abandonment may fall upon the person or persons being inflicted. This is the universal cry of those in anguish and distress. Job expresses the timeless cries of those suffering by begging God to help him understand the reason for his turmoil. One can feel the frustration and anguish as he makes the following statements as paraphrased by Waters:

> "What have I done to deserve this?" (6:24). "God, just forgive me and get it over with" (7:21). "No matter what I do, nothing changes" (chap. 9). "Why won't You answer me, God?" (10:1-7). "I can't take any more of this!" (14:18-22). "Nobody cares about me!" (19:13-22). "Where can I get some answers?" (28:12). "Everything used to be so perfect" (chap. 29). "What good is it to serve God?" (chap. 30).[109]

After dismissing all the false arguments made by his friends, Job's heart and mind finally becomes open to receive true counseling as embodied in the person of Elihu. Not only does Elihu point out that God, in fact, does care about Job, but he also shows how God's reasoning for allowing these things to happen is beyond human comprehension. In his wisdom, God was teaching Job to dismiss these false theological arguments presented by his friends as the cause of human suffering. Precisely because Job was a just and righteous man, God permitted suffering to befall him not due to any sin he had committed, but to draw Job closer to Him rather than these false arguments, which not only binds but also restricts our understanding of God. In essence, these false arguments subjected God to their morality, i.e. the morality of a give and take relationship. These theological positions would have made God the God of pragmatism, and not the God of authentic love, the God of both the righteous and the sinner. God wanted to show Job that he does reward the righteous, "but only on the basis of His love and grace."[110]

There is no better example of this than in the crucified Christ. What did Christ do to deserve such pain and suffering? We cannot even begin to imagine the level of pain Christ felt as he fell prostrate on his face and pleaded out of primordial fear, "My Father, if it is possible, let this cup pass from me ..." (Mt 26:39). Imagine the Author of Life faced with imminent death and the particular horror he must have felt when confronted with the full power of destruction and evil.[111] As the Son of God, "he experiences deeply all the horror, filth, and baseness that he must drink from the 'chalice' prepared for him: the vast power of sin and death."[112] What does it mean that the incarnate Word suffered? What does it mean for the Word to die? Finally, what does the death of the Word–made–flesh mean for suffering and death itself? We refer to this as the *mystery of the cross*. The Son of God did not die on the cross because of any theology of prosperity, but rather out of love for his Father, and most especially, for us sinners. Think about it. All Jesus wanted to do was to share the love he had with his Father with humanity, and as a consequence to his preaching, the world responded by giving him the cross. Perhaps this was the lesson God was trying to teach Job. God rewards his faithful not based on what we feel we deserve, but on the unconditional love we show towards Him and our neighbors (recall the two greatest commandments – Mt 22:37-39). In addition, God rewards the righteous not simply with earthly prosperity, but with grace and mercy.

I fully realize that this lesson is particular to Job and may not apply to all human suffering, but what does it mean for us when we believe that the Son of God, himself, suffered and died seemingly needlessly? Ultimately, this was God's answer to the very evil of suffering and death itself. Evil has been reconciled with the benevolence of God. The very meaning of suffering and death has been transformed precisely because the God–Man entered into these realities through His own suffering and death. Unable to conquer the Giver of Life, Death itself has been conquered, as St. Paul tells us: "*Where, O death, is your victory? Where, O death, is your sting?"* (1 Cor 15:55). How else are we to understand human suffering in the world unless we gaze upon the sacrifice and death of our innocent Lord as he hung upon the cruel and undeserved punishment of the cross? This is what it means to enter into the mystery of the cross: "The mystery of the Cross does not simply confront us; rather, it draws us in and gives a new value to our life."[113]

In his second volume of *Jesus of Nazareth*, Pope Benedict goes so far as to say that when we worship God with our whole existence, in the manner of the incarnate Word crucified, we become "god-like."[114] Just as Job erroneously assumed that there was some order or rationale that governed the universe other than God himself, so too did unbelievers fail to see the wisdom of the cross when brought before the wisdom of the world: "Has not God made the wisdom of the world foolish? For since in the wisdom of God the world did not come to know God through wisdom, it was the will of God through the foolishness of the proclamation to save those who have faith" (1 Cor 1:20-21). As we have seen in the case of Job, suffering unites us in a mysterious way to God himself. It is safe to say, then, that suffering endured without our eyes fixed on God is meaningless. Suffering, after all, is a condition of love; and when it is encountered in love and with faith, suffering is full of grace and redemption. We will never really know why the innocent suffer, whether the cause is of human or natural origin, but the real question posed to us is this: "What do we do when faced with suffering? Do we blame the sins of others or do we lend a helping hand? Do we exercise virtue or do we point out each other's vices?" The Christian is the one who enters into the sufferings of others, just as Christ entered into the sufferings of humanity. We must remember that if we have suffered with Christ, so too shall we be glorified with him (cf. Rom 8:17). As innocent sufferers, we too become companions of God and can look forward to the certainty of the Resurrection!

Conclusion

Since Adam and Eve, we have been in search of perfect happiness. Life is a journey of ups and downs, joys and sorrows, but we must never lose sight of the prize. Victory has already been won and the prize is within our grasp! Life is filled with skirmishes, but God never abandons his loved ones. We are sons and daughters of God. We are not orphans! We are victors![115]

When I began this book I posed the question: "Why study the faith?" The faith penetrates every aspect of our lives, from how we treat each other to how we communicate with God. Life is inseparable from what we believe. It is who we are. It is who we were made to be. Will we encounter opposition? Of course, but that is to be expected. From the foundation of the Church to its very founder, there have always been those who have opposed this way of life:

> But understand this: there will be terrifying times in the last days. People will be self-centered and lovers of money, proud, haughty, abusive, disobedient to their parents, ungrateful, irreligious, callous, implacable, slanderous, licentious, brutal, hating what is good, traitors, reckless, conceited, lovers of pleasure rather than lovers of God, as they make a pretense of religion but deny its power. Reject them (2 Tm 3:1).

For some, it is not easy to accept this truth: that we were made by God *for* God. The truth is that God deeply loves us and wants to be united with us. His greatest act of love *par excellence* was the Incarnation, whereby his only Son became man, dwelt among us, and gave up his life so that we can once again enter into paradise with the Father. Over five hundred witnessed his resurrection (cf. 1 Cor 15:6), and millions more died in his name. The Church is made up of, and continues to survive by, its witnesses – so long as its members lead by example and live a life worthy of being called "Christian." How many souls can we win over if we simply became Christ for others? There are many out there in desperate need of hope, of purpose, of redemption, and of freedom from the false teachings and destructive lifestyles proposed by this age. Many of these individuals simply don't know any better because they have never had a real encounter with the living God. Truth, the same truth Jesus proclaimed, must be made known and felt. As Timothy encourages us, "proclaim the word; be persistent whether it is convenient or inconvenient; convince, reprimand, encourage through all patience and teaching. For the time will come when people will not tolerate sound doctrine but, following their own desires and insatiable curiosity, will accumulate teachers and will stop listening to the truth and will be diverted to myths" (2 Tm 4:2).

Faith presupposes humility. Faith is acknowledging that we are not the center of the universe, though temptation seeks to tell us otherwise. People want answers, and it's this desire to know that forces us to search outside ourselves: "Today, people are looking for God not because of the order they find in the universe, but because of the disorder they find in themselves."[116] There are those who appeal to neither faith nor reason, yet it's the disorder within their lives that draws them to a higher power. Even within my own life I have questioned why God allows certain things to happen, and time and time again I have discovered that many of my own failings have come from relying on my own efforts, rather than placing my intentions before the altar of the Lamb who has my best interests at heart. It takes great humility to accept the reality that alone I am nothing and that success comes when I am dependent on another. As I reflect upon this, the image that comes to mind is that of St. John at the Last Supper reclining his head on the bosom of the Lord.

Throughout this book we have covered a lot of theology, morality, spirituality, and a variety of things in between, but at the end of it all, the most important and essential element is the personal relationship one has with the living God. We have viewed God as Creator, Father, Savior, and Redeemer, but do we view him as friend? It may seem strange, but friendship is one of the most intimate levels that can occur between two persons. When we look back at our lives, from infancy to adulthood, how has our image of God changed? When we were children, perhaps we saw God as "Father." As we began to know more about the world around us, perhaps our image of God changed to that of "Creator." And as we received some type of religious education and learned about the person of Jesus, perhaps our image of God shifted to that of "Savior." While all these views are accurate descriptions of God, somewhere along the way, for a lot of people, the image of God has progressively grown less personal. For a large majority of adults, the most intimate they have ever been with God was when they were children and God was "Father." As adults, many struggle with intimacy with God because they simply don't know how to relate with Him.

I believe part of the problem is, that as adults, we struggle to find an image of God that combines the innocence of our infancy with the experience that comes with growing up. We don't necessarily want to regress to a state of infancy when we approach God, and we don't want to pretend to be someone we are not. The truth is God wants us to approach him just as we are. He has been with us at every stage of our lives even if we haven't been aware of it. He is very much like a close friend that we grew up with; a person doesn't approach an old friend the same way they did when they were children. If they did, the relationship would cease to be relevant. We must relate with God as we are.

What does it mean, then, to have a personal relationship with God? To have a personal relationship with God is to invite God into every aspect of my life: my work, my family, my likes, my dislikes, etc. After all, aren't these the things we normally discuss with our friends? Why should it be different with God? What reason is there to feel embarrassed? Doesn't God know me better than I know myself? It is important to invite Christ even into the ordinary aspects of our lives. For example, other than sharing with Jesus my struggles and problems, do I share with him the type of music that I listen to, or the people I like spending time with, or the activities I enjoy doing? It may sound strange at first, but this is no different than how we would relate with any other person. I think part of the problem is that we don't see God as friend, but rather as an other-worldly being, whose omnipotence intimidates us, and therefore makes it hard for us to relate to. Jesus became man precisely so that we may experience him in the flesh, as one of us. Jesus established relationships with his disciples as a human being: he ate with them, he drank with them, he prayed with them, and he wept with them.

One of the most concrete ways in which we experience Christ is through community – by being and interacting with others who share the faith. This is what it means to be a part of the Body of Christ. One cannot hope to belong to the Mystical Body of Christ without gathering and worshipping as one family in faith. If the Good Lord had intended for us to practice our faith privately he would not have established a community of believers. The greatest manifestation of this is the celebration of the Eucharist. The Mass gives us a glimpse of the larger community that is the Church. Sometimes we tend to forget that by virtue of our Baptism we enter into a larger family. At the same time, however, it can be easy to attend Mass and still be disconnected from the rest of the faith community. An individual cannot attend Mass and not feel empathy for the one sitting beside them. The Mass was never intended as a personal form of worship. From the beginning of the early Church, when the Eucharist was celebrated in people's homes, the faithful felt a sense of belongingness when gathered together, especially during persecutions. When a stomach feels pain, it hurts the whole body. When the stomach is healed, the whole body becomes healthy. The community of faith strengthens our own faith - strength in numbers so-to-speak.

Above all, the source of our strength is the Eucharist itself, the real Body and Blood of Christ. The Eucharist draws us in (*communion*), and then sends us out (*mission*). We gather strength from the Body and Blood of Christ as it becomes one with our own. We become tabernacles of the Most High:

The communion rail is a place of exchange. The people give time and receive eternity; they give self-denial and receive life; they give nothingness and receive all. Holy Communion commits each to a closer union not only with Christ's life, but also with His death—to greater detachment from the world, to surrender of luxuries for the sake of the poor, to death of the old Adam for rebirth in Christ, the new Adam.[117]

We are thus called to take Christ back to our homes, to our work, to our schools, and to the day-to-day encounters with the rest of humanity. We are not called to proselytize (to impose our religion on others), but rather to bear witness to the faith by our actions. As Pope Paul VI observed, "Modern man listens more willingly to witnesses than to teachers, and if he does listen to teachers, it is because they are witnesses" (*Evangelii Nuntiandi*, par. 41). It is our witness as imitators of Christ that will draw others to Christ himself. The rest is left to the Spirit, because ultimately, it is the work of the Spirit that moves hearts.

Will there be people who won't understand us? Yes. Will there be people who disagree with our beliefs? Undoubtedly. Will we be persecuted? Possibly. But this is nothing new. Jesus was hated by the world from the very beginning: "If the world hates you, realize that it hated me first" (Jn 15:18). Amidst the animosity that we may encounter, it is important to recall the words of St. Paul to the Romans:

What will separate us from the love of Christ? Will anguish, or distress, or persecution, or famine, or nakedness, or peril, or the sword?...No, in all these things we conquer overwhelmingly through him who loved us. For I am convinced that neither death, nor life, nor angels, nor principalities, nor present things, nor future things, nor powers, nor height, nor depth, nor any other creature will be able to separate us from the love of God in Christ Jesus our Lord (Rom 8:37-39).

When we have Christ in us we realize that everything else becomes less important in comparison. Things we once wanted now seem less important. The measure of success is no longer what the world proclaims (money, power, lust), but the intimacy we foster with Christ. As Archbishop Fulton Sheen once said: "It is ever true that the richer a soul is on the inside, the less need it has of luxuries on the outside. Excessive adornments and an inordinate love of comforts are proofs of our inner nakedness."[118]

When we look back at the *Parable of the Sower* (cf. Mt. 13:4) we have to ask ourselves, "which seed do I want to be?" Will I be the seed that fell at the edge of the path, the one who received the word of God without desiring to understand it? Or the seed that landed on rocky ground, the one who accepted the word of God with joy but at the first wave of trials abandoned it because they had no root? Or will I be the seed that landed in thorns, the one who hears the word of God but is chocked up by the worries and riches of the world? Or finally, will I be the seed that landed on rich soil, the one who received the word of God, understood it, and now produces much fruit?

There will come a point in every disciple's life where Jesus will stop and ask us, "who do *you* say that I am?" Will we be able to answer as Peter did (cf. Mt. 16:16)? It is very easy to conceptually like something, to like the *idea* of something, but it's another matter entirely to integrate it and make it a part of one's own life. It's like that moment when Jesus told his disciples that, "unless you eat the flesh of the Son of Man and drink his blood, you do not have life within you" (Jn 6:53). Will we be like those disciples that left him because they couldn't accept this teaching, because they could not eat his flesh and drink his blood? Or will we respond as Peter did: "Master, to whom shall we go? You have the words of eternal life" (Jn 6:68)? Are we willing to integrate the body and blood of Christ with our own? Are we willing to contribute to the community of believers, his Mystical Body? These are all important questions, but the ultimate question we must each answer is the following: "What kind of disciple do *you* want to be?"

Endnotes

[1] J.R.R. Tolkien, *The Silmarillion* (New York: Houghton Mifflin Company, 2004), p. xix.

[2] Tolkien, *The Silmarillion*, p. xix.

[3] New Jerusalem Bible, "Exodus," in *The New Jerusalem Bible* notes (New York, NY: Doubleday, 1985), p. 83.

[4] cf. *Catechism of the Catholic Church*, 2nd ed. (Washington, D.C.: United States Catholic Conference, 2000), no. 438.

[5] cf. *Catechism of the Catholic Church*, 2nd ed., no. 439.

[6] Joseph Ratzinger, *Jesus of Nazareth: From the Entrance into Jerusalem to the Resurrection*, trans. Philip J. Whitmore (San Francisco: Ignatius Press, 2011), p. 203.

[7] Joseph Ratzinger, *Jesus of Nazareth: From the Baptism in the River Jordan to the Transfiguration*, trans. Adrian J. Walker (New York: Doubleday, 2007), p. 22.

[8] Ratzinger, *Jesus of Nazareth: From the Baptism in the River Jordan to the Transfiguration*, p. 26.

[9] Ratzinger, *Jesus of Nazareth: From the Baptism in the River Jordan to the Transfiguration*, p. 328.

[10] Ratzinger, *Jesus of Nazareth: From the Entrance into Jerusalem to the Resurrection*, p. 203.

[11] cf. *Catechism of the Catholic Church*, 2nd ed., no. 440.

[12] Ratzinger, *Jesus of Nazareth: From the Baptism in the River Jordan to the Transfiguration*, p. 40.

[13] cf. Thomas Aquinas, *Summa Theologiae*, III, q. 86, a. 1.

[14] cf. *Catechism of the Catholic Church*, 2nd ed., no. 1502.

[15] *Catechism of the Catholic Church*, 2nd ed., no. 1324.

[16] cf. *Catechism of the Catholic Church*, 2nd ed., no. 1322.

[17] Humphrey Carpenter, *The Letters of J.R.R. Tolkien* (New York: Houghton Mifflin Harcourt, 2000), p. 53.

[18] cf. *Catechism of the Catholic Church*, 2nd ed., no. 1211.

[19] *Catechism of the Catholic Church*, 2nd ed., no. 1285.

[20] cf. *Catechism of the Catholic Church*, 2nd ed., no. 1288.

[21] cf. *Catechism of the Catholic Church*, 2nd ed., no. 1289.

[22] cf. *Catechism of the Catholic Church*, 2nd ed., no. 1303, & Is 11: 1-4.

[23] cf. Augustine, *Confessions*, trans. by Henry Chadwick (Oxford: Oxford University Press, 1991), p. 25.
"The single desire that dominated my search for delight was simply to love and to be loved."

[24] cf. Dietrich von Hildebrand, *Marriage: The Mystery of Faithful Love* (Manchester, New Hampshire: Sophia Institute Press, 1984), p. x.

[25] cf. Augustine, *Confessions*, pp. 23, 25.
During Augustine's youth, he shares how he was easily swayed by worldly pleasures: "My sin consisted in this, that I sought pleasure, sublimity, and truth not in God but in his creatures, in myself and other created beings. So it was that I plunged into miseries, confusions, and errors" (Augustine, *Confessions*, p. 23). Again he shares: "I turned from unity in you to be lost in multiplicity" (Augustine, *Confessions*, p. 25).

[26] cf. Augustine, *Confessions*, p. 25; Donald H. Calloway, MIC, *The Virgin Mary and Theology of the Body* (West Chester, Pennsylvania: Ascension Press, 2005), p. 43.
Augustine struggled during his puberty, as do many of us today, to differentiate moments of love and lust: "The Bubbling impulses of puberty befogged and obscured my heart so that it could not see the difference between love's serenity

and lust's darkness" (Augustine, *Confessions*, p. 25). In regards to St. Joseph's relationship with Mary, we see the model of Christian Marriage from the husband's point of view as he observes chastity within the marriage: "Due to the grace of the Holy Spirit, this commitment does not eviscerate his conjugal feelings for his wife but, rather, elevates and purifies them" (Calloway, *The Virgin Mary*, p. 43).

[27] cf. Augustine, *Confessions*, pp. 20, 38.
Confronted by the corruption of those around him, we see a similar parallel with the society that surrounded Augustine and ours today. He describes how men took pleasure in objectifying women and boasted of their sexual conquests using eloquent speech: "But if they described their lusts in a rich vocabulary of well constructed prose with a copious and ornate style, they received praise and congratulated themselves" (Augustine, *Confessions*, p. 20). This eventually led him to say the following: "The blindness of humanity is so great that people are actually proud of their blindness" (Augustine, *Confessions*, p. 38).

[28] cf. Augustine, *Confessions*, p. 47.
"...when men either corrupt or pervert their own nature which you made and ordered, or when people immoderately use what is allowed, turning to what is forbidden, they indulge a burning lust for 'that use which is contrary to nature" (Augustine, *Confessions*, p. 47).

[29] Augustine, *Confessions*, p. 110.
Through Augustine's own mistakes he teaches us the way to truly view the world: "For I was so submerged and blinded that I could not think of the light of moral goodness and of a beauty to be embraced for its own sake – beauty seen not by the eye of the flesh, but only by inward discernment" (Augustine, *Confessions*, p. 110).

[30] cf. Dietrich von Hildebrand, *Marriage: The Mystery of Faithful Love*, p. 5.
"... marriage is the closest and most intimate of all earthly unions in which, more than in any other, one person gives himself to another without reserve, where the other in his complete personality is the object of love, and where mutual love is in a specific way the theme (that is to say, the core) of the relationship" (Hildebrand, *Marriage: The Mystery of Faithful Love*, p. 5).

[31] cf. Benedict XVI, *Light of the World: The Pope, the Church, and the Signs of the Times*, trans. Michael J. Miller & Adrian J. Walker (San Francisco: Ignatius Press, 2010), p. 46.
In his chapter confronting atheism and agnosticism, Pope Benedict XVI addresses those who refuse to acknowledge the faith because of their egotism. They prefer to

remain in a comfortable lifestyle that causes them to care only about themselves: "People are accustomed to a particular sort of life, and when this is threatened, they of course put up resistance" (Benedict XVI, *Light of the World*, p. 46).

[32] cf. Paul Haffner, *The Sacramental Mystery* (Leominster, Herefordshire: Gracewing, 1999), p. 234

Here I allude to Canon 1055, which defines marriage. Haffner summarizes Canon 1055 based on the Genesis account: "The union of man and woman was characterized by unity and indissolubility (Gn 2:24), and orientated towards procreation (Gn 1:28). Although it was given to human beings from their very nature, it still implied something sacred, since God blessed Adam and Eve (Gn 1:28)" (Paul Haffner, *The Sacramental Mystery*, p. 234).

[33] cf. Immanuel Kant, *Critique of Practical Reason*, trans. Norman Kemp Smith (New York: Humanities Press, 1950), p. 93.

Here I refer to Kant's "Categorical Imperative" for the governance of a just society, where he succeeds in removing metaphysics and religion from the equation: "Act only according to that maxim by which you can at the same time will that it should become a universal law" (Kant, *Critique of Practical Reason*, p. 93). However, his notion of the Categorical Imperative is not an original thought. Jesus' Golden Rule of "treat others as you would like them to treat you" (Mt 7:12) predates Kant's Categorical Imperative by over sixteen hundred years.

[34] cf. Michael J. Sandel, *Justice: What's the Right Thing to Do?* (New York: Farrar, Straus and Giroux 2009), p. 107.

Although Kant was a Christian, he did "not base morality on divine authority. He argues instead that we can arrive at the supreme principle of morality through the exercise of what he calls 'pure practical reason'" (Sandel, *Justice*, p. 107). His transcendence is not aimed towards God but towards humanity as a whole, in which every individual is an end in itself. By following the binding contract of marriage (in line with the notion of pure practical reason), a good marriage, on strictly practical reasons, becomes a good example for the rest of humanity. This is to say that my marriage is an example for the good of humanity because I do not treat my wife as a thing for my own satisfaction and neither does she treat me as a thing. She is an end to herself and I am an end to myself. This allows us, according to Kant, to preserve our dignity and have mutual respect towards each other. This is very similar to Augustine's view of marriage except that it is God who makes it whole and gives it meaning, whereas for Kant, what makes marriage whole and valuable is that it contributes to the good of humanity. Kant's moral values lie not in the realm of metaphysics but in the realm of practicality.

[35] cf. Waldstein, Intro to Pope John Paul II's *Man and Woman He Created Them: A Theology of the Body* (Boston, MA: Pauline Books & Media, 2006), p. 46.
Here we see the contrasting argument against Kant's Categorical Imperative: "All metaphysical topics such as love and justice are not founded on reason because they cannot be reasoned by Kant's transcendental elements, "as a theoretical science, it is completely limited to the realm of appearances based on received sense-data" (Waldstein, Intro to *Man and Woman*, p. 46). In other words, Kant limits love to its strictly practical aspects and makes it devoid of any further meaning.

[36] cf. Hildebrand, *Marriage: The Mystery of Faithful Love*, p. 8.
"It is true that in every kind of love one gives oneself in one way or another, but here the giving is literally complete and ultimate. Not only the heart but the entire personality is given up to the other. When a man and a woman love each other in this way, they give themselves to each other at the very moment they begin to love" (Hildebrand, *Marriage: The Mystery of Faithful Love*, p. 8).

[37] cf. Julián Marías, *The Philosophy of Gabriel Marcel*, Trans. By Josefina I. Frondizi (Southern Illinois University, Carbondale: The Library of Living Philosophers, 1984), p. 555.
In Gabriel Marcel's phenomenology, he explains the importance of love and faith and why the two cannot be separated: "And so, side by side with faith we posit love I have said elsewhere that love is the condition of faith, and in a sense this is true. But it is only one aspect. I believe that in reality love and faith cannot be dissociated. When faith ceases to be love it congeals into objective belief in a power that is conceived more or less physically. And love which is not faith (which does not posit the transcendence of the God that is loved) is only a sort of abstract game" (Julián Marías, *The Philosophy of Gabriel Marcel*, p. 557).

[38] cf. Marías, *The Philosophy of Gabriel Marcel*, p. 557.
For Marcel, as well as for Augustine, love ultimately points to the eternal, God: "In this sense it is true to say that love only addresses itself to what is eternal, it immobilizes the beloved beyond the world of genesis and vicissitude" (Marías, *The Philosophy of Gabriel Marcel*, p. 557).

[39] cf. *Catechism of the Catholic Church*, 2nd ed., no. 1536.

[40] Ratzinger, *Jesus of Nazareth: From the Entrance into Jerusalem to the Resurrection*, p. 151.

[41] cf. Exodus 3:14

[42] Ratzinger, *Jesus of Nazareth: From the Baptism in the River Jordan to the Transfiguration*, p. 41.

[43] cf. International Committee on English in the Liturgy, *General Instruction of the Roman Missal*, Third Typical ed. (Washington, D.C.: United States Conference of Catholic Bishops, 2002), no. 4.

[44] cf. Pope John Paul II, *Man and Woman He Created Them: A Theology of the Body*, pp. 476, 478.

[45] cf. Second Vatican Council, *Sacrosanctum Concilium*, Constitution on the Sacred Liturgy, December 4, 1963, no. 7.

[46] cf. Second Vatican Council, *Gaudium et Spes*, Pastoral Constitution on the Church in the Modern World, December 7, 1965, no. 48.

[47] *Catechism of the Catholic Church*, 2nd ed., no. 1619.

[48] *Catechism of the Catholic Church*, 2nd ed., no. 1620.

[49] Second Vatican Council, *Sacrosanctum Concilium*, no. 7.

[50] *Catechism of the Catholic Church*, 2nd ed., no. 916.

[51] Ratzinger, *Jesus of Nazareth: From the Baptism in the River Jordan to the Transfiguration*, p. 99.

[52] Ratzinger, *Jesus of Nazareth: From the Entrance into Jerusalem to the Resurrection*, p. 55.

[53] Ratzinger, *Jesus of Nazareth: From the Entrance into Jerusalem to the Resurrection*, p. 55.

[54] John Paul II, *Man and Woman He Created Them: A Theology of the Body*, p. 481.

[55] cf. Ratzinger, *Jesus of Nazareth: From the Entrance into Jerusalem to the Resurrection*, p. 211.

[56] cf. Lk 2:35

[57] Ratzinger, *Jesus of Nazareth: From the Entrance into Jerusalem to the Resurrection*, p. 211.

[58] Ratzinger, *Jesus of Nazareth: From the Baptism in the River Jordan to the Transfiguration*, p. 27.

[59] Ratzinger, *Jesus of Nazareth: From the Baptism in the River Jordan to the Transfiguration*, p. 30.

[60] Ratzinger, *Jesus of Nazareth: From the Baptism in the River Jordan to the Transfiguration*, p. 30.

[61] Ratzinger, *Jesus of Nazareth: From the Baptism in the River Jordan to the Transfiguration*, p. 37.

[62] Ratzinger, *Jesus of Nazareth: From the Baptism in the River Jordan to the Transfiguration*, p. 38.

[63] Fulton Sheen, "Ages of Man and Temptation," Volume 1: *Love is Faith*, DVD, prod. Sheen Productions (Worcestar, PA: Distributed by Vision Video, 2007).

[64] Fulton Sheen, "Ages of Man and Temptation," Volume 1: *Love is Faith*.

[65] cf. Timothy M. Gallagher, *The Discernment of Spirits* (Chestnut Ridge, NY: The Crossroad Publishing Company, 2005), pp. 34, 35.

[66] cf. Mk 5:9

[67] Fulton Sheen, "Ages of Man and Temptation," Volume 1: *Love is Faith*.

[68] Ratzinger, *Jesus of Nazareth: From the Baptism in the River Jordan to the Transfiguration*, p. 100.

[69] Ratzinger, *Jesus of Nazareth: From the Baptism in the River Jordan to the Transfiguration*, p. 28.

[70] cf. *Catechism of the Catholic Church*, 2nd ed., no. 2730.

[71] *Catechism of the Catholic Church*, 2nd ed., no. 2725.

[72] *Catechism of the Catholic Church*, 2nd ed., no. 2725.

[73] *Catechism of the Catholic Church*, 2nd ed., no. 2726.

[74] cf. *Catechism of the Catholic Church*, 2nd ed., no. 2727.

[75] Augustine, *Confessions*, p. 3.

[76] cf. *Catechism of the Catholic Church*, 2nd ed., no. 2728.

[77] *Catechism of the Catholic Church*, 2nd ed., no. 2728.

[78] Augustine, *Confessions*, p. 201.

[79] *Catechism of the Catholic Church*, 2nd ed., no. 2731.

[80] cf. Gallagher, *The Discernment of Spirits,* pp. 60,63.

[81] cf. Gallagher, *The Discernment of Spirits,* p. 74.

[82] Benedict XVI, *Light of the World: The Pope, the Church, and the Signs of the Times,* trans. Michael J. Miller & Adrian J. Walker (San Francisco: Ignatius Press, 2010), p.46.

[83] Fulton Sheen, *The Priest Is Not His Own* (New York, McGraw Hill Book Company, 1963), p. 111.

[84] Sheen, *The Priest Is Not His Own,* p. 111.

[85] Ratzinger, *Jesus of Nazareth: From the Baptism in the River Jordan to the Transfiguration,* p. 33.

[86] Ratzinger, *Jesus of Nazareth: From the Baptism in the River Jordan to the Transfiguration,* p. 35.

[87] Pope Francis, "Morning Meditation in the Chapel of the Domus Sanctae Marthae: *Two Coats of Paint,"* *L'Osservatore Romano,* Weekly ed. in English, 14 November 2014, n. 46.

[88] Robert W. Finn, "Homily for the Eve of the Election," *The Catholic Key Blog,* 3 November 2008, http://catholickey.blogspot.com/2008/11/bishop-finns-election-eve-homily.html (1 September 2015).

[89] Number of Abortions – Abortion Counters, "US Since 1973: Roe vs Wade," http://www.numberofabortions.com (1 September 2015).

[90] Meg Ray, "The Downside of Cohabitating Before Marriage," *New York Times*, 14 April 2012, http://www.nytimes.com/2012/04/15/opinion/sunday/the-downside-of-cohabiting-before-marriage.html?_r=1& (April 15, 2012).

[91] *Catechism of the Catholic Church*, 2nd ed., no. 2337.

[92] cf. *Catechism of the Catholic Church*, 2nd ed., no. 2338.

[93] Bishop Victor Galeone, *Marriage: A Communion of Life and Love* (Cincinnati OH, The Couple to Couple League International, Inc., 1995), p. 3

[94] Joseph Ratzinger, *Christianity and The Crises of Cultures*, trans. Brian McNeil (San Francisco: Ignatius Press, 2006), p. 52.

[95] Ratzinger, *Christianity and The Crises of Cultures*, p. 65.

[96] Robert Johann, "Love and Justice", Ethics and Society: Original Essays on Contemporary Moral Problems, ed. Richard de George (Garden City, Doubleday, 1966), pp. 41-47.

[97] Ratzinger, *Jesus of Nazareth: From the Baptism in the River Jordan to the Transfiguration*, p. 33.

[98] Ratzinger, *Jesus of Nazareth: From the Baptism in the River Jordan to the Transfiguration*, p. 33.

[99] This last paragraph was inspired by a conference given by Fr. Ferdinand Santos, Ph.D., to a group of deacon-elects on April 14, 2014.

[100] John Paul II, *Fides et Ratio*, Encyclical Letter on the Relationship Between Faith & Reason (Boston, MA: Pauline Books, 1998), p. 7.

[101] cf. Robert J. Spitzer, *New Proofs for the Existence of God* (Grand Rapids, Michigan: Wm. B. Eerdmans Publishing Co., 2010), p. 16.

[102] cf. Spitzer, *New Proofs for the Existence of God*, p. 13.

[103] Stephen W. Hawking and Leonard Mlodinow, *The Grand Design* (New York: Bantam Book, 2010), p. 172.

[104] Spitzer, *New Proofs for the Existence of God*, p. 59.

[105] Larry J. Waters, "Reflections On Suffering From the Book of Job," *Bibliotheca Sacra* 154 (October–December 1997): 436–51, p. 438.

[106] Larry J. Waters, "Reflections On Suffering From the Book of Job," *Bibliotheca Sacra* 154, p. 441.

[107] cf. Larry J. Waters, "Reflections On Suffering From the Book of Job," *Bibliotheca Sacra* 154, p. 441.

[108] Larry J. Waters, "Reflections On Suffering From the Book of Job," *Bibliotheca Sacra* 154, p. 442.

[109] Larry J. Waters, "Reflections On Suffering From the Book of Job," *Bibliotheca Sacra* 154, p. 443.

[110] Larry J. Waters, "Reflections On Suffering From the Book of Job," *Bibliotheca Sacra* 154, p. 445.

[111] cf. Ratzinger, *Jesus of Nazareth: From the Entrance into Jerusalem to the Resurrection*, p. 155.

[112] Ratzinger, *Jesus of Nazareth: From the Entrance into Jerusalem to the Resurrection*, p. 155.

[113] Ratzinger, *Jesus of Nazareth: From the Entrance into Jerusalem to the Resurrection*, p. 236.

[114] Ratzinger, *Jesus of Nazareth: From the Entrance into Jerusalem to the Resurrection*, p. 236.

[115] cf. Dr. Carol Razza, *Pastoral Counseling II*, (St. Vincent de Paul Regional Seminary, Fall 2014).

[116] Sheen, *The Priest Is Not His Own*, pp. 63–64.

[117] Sheen, *The Priest Is Not His Own*, p. 20.

[118] Sheen, *The Priest Is Not His Own*, p. 13.

Printed in the United States
By Bookmasters